Post 381

The Memoirs of a
Belfast Air Raid Warden

by

James Doherty

FRIAR'S BUSH PRESS

Illustrations

The cover is based on a painting by Thomas A. Crawley which was purchased by the Belfast Museum and Art Gallery at a Belfast civil defence exhibition in 1943.

Acknowledgements

We are grateful to the Ulster Museum for the loan of the cover picture and for granting permission to use the photographs from the Garland Collection. Thanks are also due to Mr R. C. Ludgate for the use of the photograph of the Salisbury Avenue tram depot and to Mr M. Bailey for the photograph of the International Bar.

Contents

The wardens of Post 381, April, 1941.   (Doherty Collection)
*This photograph was taken at St Malachy's College where the post was based
temporarily owing to damage at their post nearby in Cranburn Street.*
*Included are the author James Doherty, James Howey and Victor McQuillan (all
founder members of Post 381) and Norman Shrage, Matthew McKenna, Jack McGlad-
dery, William Trainor, Joseph O'Brien and the Group Warden Brian Gillespie, seen on
the right with his hand on the handle of a stirrup pump. The author is seated in the
centre, next to Brian Gillespie.*

Introduction

This is the story of the Home Front in Belfast in the Second
World War. It is the story of the people and the volunteers who
served in the civil defence or A.R.P. (air raid precautions) as it
was more generally known.

Such a record as this is necessary lest in the welter of
published material, dealing with air force operations, land and
sea engagements, espionage, resistance and D Day memories,
the history of the Home Front is forgotten or that myths
replace facts.

It was not only air raids and terrible living conditions that
the civilian population had to endure. There were all the other
rigours of war, the shortages and disruption of basic amenities
and the constant battle to provide that the housewife experienced
on the kitchen front. The evacuation of children was akin to a
bereavement where families were totally unused to separation.

In spite of the trials of the time I have not hesitated to
mention the moments of humour I witnessed even at times of
greatest stress. I found that this was often a natural reaction
which helped people to cope with what otherwise would have
been hopeless situations. Ulster wit is hard to suppress and
brightened the worst situations.

In compiling this first history of the civil defence and Home
Front in Ulster I was, unlike many other researchers, fortunate
in having first hand experience and information concerning
the most restricted, censored material; much of the written
record has been lost or destroyed. The source of my information is my own memory, memos, letters, photographs and
now rare documents which I preserved as souvenirs. I have
endeavoured to tell the story through the experience of the
group of wardens with whom I had the honour to serve.

In many cases I was the only civilian to witness the most horrific and censored incidents which are still surrounded by rumour and conjecture. These include the death and destruction which took place at Victoria Barracks: together with another warden I was the only civilian who was permitted to see the effects of the air raid. I can also tell from first-hand experience the grim details about how the Falls Road Baths was used as a morgue and the story of an American air force plane crash which has been shrouded in secrecy. There is also the untold record of a group of Northern Ireland wardens who volunteered to serve in London during the flying bomb and rocket attacks which terrorised that city towards the end of the war.

I have tried to give some idea of the formation, training and other pursuits of the civil defence. A point which is sometimes forgotten and which must be emphasised is that service in the civil defence was voluntary in Northern Ireland and, unlike the service in Britain, volunteers could leave when they wished. Those who maintained their loyalty to the service were bound together by their personal dedication and love of their city and community.

I have looked briefly at the neglect of proper planning and provision of adequate equipment for the defence of Belfast, which should have been considered one of the most important cities in its contribution towards the war effort.

The book is based on my own experiences and that of my companions. However, it is also the story of the people of Belfast. I was there among the people as part of the community. Everyone has a memory of the war years. It may be of their own experiences or fragments of conversation heard when they were children. Whatever may be the case, I hope that these memories will be stirred by this book. For those too young to remember, I trust it will help to form some idea of life in war-time Ulster.

I hope that I have helped to record the tremendous tasks undertaken by the civil defence for those who lived through the war years. Above all, I dedicate this work to the small group of men and women who, without proper equipment and little regard for their own safety, faced the most savage and prolonged single attack on any city in the United Kingdom. This is their story.

1 Preparations for war

I was born on St Valentine's Day, 14th February, 1920, in Nelson Street and I grew up in that part of North Belfast known as Little Italy because of the presence of immigrant families. It was an area of back-to-back terraced houses, the homes of mill workers, dock workers, seamen and tradesmen. After the First World War, times were hard and unemployment was common, but it was a close knit, settled community.

During my years at school, memories of the Great War were fresh. Instead of cowboys and indians, we preferred to play soldiers, with Germany as the enemy. When I left school in 1936, fears of another major war were already building in people's minds. People were anxious about the future and feared for their husbands and sons, but no one thought that their own streets would be devastated in a very few years time.

In 1936 I took up an apprenticeship as a trainee upholsterer with a firm in Percy Street. As I went about my work, fears of another war continued to grow as contrasting European ideologies clashed in the fury of the Spanish Civil War. The following years passed in an atmosphere of German expansionism, international tension and diplomatic manoeuvre as the British prime minister, Neville Chamberlain, struggled in vain to avoid the conflict which today seems to have been inevitable all along. This was not how the public saw it at the time: a poll conducted in Britain only days before the war is reported to have found that only 18% believed that there would be a war.

It was in this background that the first images of civil defence were born and why, to this day, it is associated with gas masks. The public was directed as early as 1938 to go to various centres, usually church halls and schools, to be fitted

1

and supplied with a gas mask or respirator, as they were officially known. This was during the Czechoslovakian crisis before Chamberlain's agreement with Hitler at Munich. Over 40 million people were tested and fitted by volunteers throughout the United Kingdom, a mammoth task. This first contact with the A.R.P. (air raid precautions) left a lasting impression. There are still many gas masks hidden away in attics. The unearthing of these old souvenirs causes great excitement especially among the younger members of the family and revives memories as parents and grandparents relive nights spent in shelters clutching their respirators.

The gas masks came as a shock to the nation. Thousands and perhaps millions never attempted to put them on again after the initial experience, which was certainly not a pleasant one. Respirators were considered to be of great importance for the safety of the entire population. Intelligence reports had suggested that gas would be the weapon used against the civil population and it was strongly emphasised that people should practise using their masks at home and carry them with them when they went out. As well as the fear of the mask itself there was the terrible thought of our cities, our streets and even our homes being subjected to a choking poison gas attack. One could imagine the gas creeping through our streets like a thick fog and it was all very frightening. Older people had vivid memories of seeing husbands, sons or brothers slowly dying as a result of gas attacks in the trenches during the 1914 war.

New-born babies were supplied with special respirators which resembled the helmets we now associate with spacemen's suits. Young mothers, understandably, panicked at the thought of having to use them. In the event of a gas attack a parent would have had to put the baby into the helmet and to ensure that the baby had an adequate air supply which was maintained by means of a built-in hand bellows. Under such circumstances as were experienced during the blitz this would have been extremely difficult and grave doubts must have arisen among those responsible for anti-gas measures.

The children, always ready to adjust themselves, introduced the gas mask into their world of make believe and play. They skipped and played ball games to the rhythm of a parody based on a well known community song which went something like this:

> Underneath the spreading chestnut tree
> Mr Chamberlain said to me
> 'If you want to get your gas mask free
> Go and see the A.R.P.'

For the children there was something special about growing up during the war years. Birthdays from schooldays onward were marked by the changing of their respirators. The baby helmet was changed for a young child's Mickey Mouse mask. These were gaily coloured to make them less frightening to young children. At a later date the Mickey Mouse was exchanged for a small size civilian type mask and so on through to a medium, and if necessary a large size.

The wardens were so closely involved in the distribution and maintenance of the masks that, looking back, it seems obvious why the two are still so closely associated in people's minds even today.

The last months of peace in Europe dragged from one crisis to another as Hitler's territorial claims threatened Poland. The invasion of Poland by Germany was followed by a British ultimatum. While the whole country listened, the prime minister broadcast to the nation on Sunday 3rd September 1939. They all heard the fateful words, 'This country is now at war with Germany'. As the prime minister finished his statement, sirens wailed out, the warning of enemy aircraft approaching. In the few minutes before the all clear sounded, there was time in the confusion for everyone to realise that the whole civilian population was now under threat.

In the early months of the war, inactivity on both sides led to a period known as the 'Phoney War'. This was when the A.R.P. personnel took most stick. They distributed pamphlets which gave instructions on how to prepare a shelter in the home or garden, what to do in the event of an air raid, first aid and fire fighting. In the rosy days of the phoney war the public took little interest; to them it all seemed as unrealistic as the mock air raid exercises carried out by wardens and ambulance personnel with make-believe casualties.

The need to have an efficient and well equipped A.R.P.

service became more urgent as the war developed. The public response to renewed recruiting drives continued to be steady. I was now nineteen and had some experience of working in the community with a church organisation. Civil defence seemed important, so I volunteered along with my friends. We attended a general course and then made our choice of section.

Initial courses were based on anti-gas training. The fear that gas would be used as a weapon continued right through the war, although training was revised from time to time.

On completion of the initial courses which lasted about six weeks, recruits could choose the section in which they wished to serve. The rescue, ambulance and auxiliary fire service were the most popular. The other sections, air raid wardens, welfare and headquarters staff were the Cinderellas of the civil defence corps. They lacked the glamour of the mobile sections and recruitment was slow.

My friends and I joined the wardens' section and on making enquiries we learned that there was no organised wardens' post in the immediate area, so we asked for permission to form our own group. The wardens were unlike the other sections which operated from central depots. The basic principle of the wardens was to operate locally at all times. They were expected to be thoroughly acquainted with their area and residents, and to identify themselves closely with the community.

Our first meeting was a solemn and important occasion. As we saw it we were taking upon ourselves the responsibility for one of the most significant and vulnerable areas in the whole city. It bordered on Sailortown and part of the docks; the York Street mill area and a maze of densely populated streets; in fact North Belfast from York Street to Duncairn Gardens/Antrim Road. There were nine wardens at the first meeting: James Howey, Joseph and Victor McQuillan, Dennis Kelly, Frank Arthurs, Billy Edwards, Thomas Marlow, James Doherty and ex-Sergeant-major Murphy. Marlowe, Edwards and Murphy were ex-army and we elected them to be the officers.

Sergeant Murphy's house became our temporary headquarters. We met there and studied pamphlets on the duties and training of air raid wardens. At this time it was very difficult to see ourselves in the role we were to fill.

Edwards was in charge of equipment, although at first we did not even have an armband to identify us as wardens. A few weeks later at our usual training session Edwards produced a large carton containing helmets, armbands and respirators complete with haversacks. It was a memorable evening. We were like a bunch of children, keen and excited. We slung our haversacks, donned our helmets, put on our armbands and lined up for inspection in front of the Sergeant-major or Group Warden as he now was. He must have thought we were a scruffy lot as we stood before him, in all shapes and sizes and varieties of clothing: not a regimental turnout I can assure you! He congratulated us on our smart appearance and then came the highlight of the evening. He unrolled a large map of the area which was marked off in sections. After a briefing on our patrol areas, we split up into groups and went out on our first blackout patrol.

It was these first faltering steps and the close comradeship that existed within the ranks of those early volunteers that helped to give the organisation the spirit and determination to carry out the almost impossible tasks which were to confront it later.

Our first post was an old disused shop but it gave us a feeling of importance and excitement ran high. At last we had a wardens' post in our own area. We were not alone in being given old dilapidated premises; it was in similar buildings throughout the city that wardens' posts were located.

Shortly after the setting up of the new post, three new officers were appointed by district headquarters to take over the administration of the post area. They were keen and enthusiastic and had attended special courses to qualify for the positions. Under their leadership we started to train with the aim of becoming the efficient wardens we had pictured when we read the early training pamphlets at the Sergeant's house.

Our training sessions covered damage assessment and reporting procedures, stirrup pump drills, basic rescue, first aid and stretcher drill as well as fire fighting, a specially exciting part of the training. This new knowledge gave us a sense of purpose and confidence. We knew that if we were called upon we could use these skills in the service of the public.

Recruitment was slow but we were getting some good volunteers. They arrived from different parts of our scattered area and instead of our original nine we later had over two dozen. It would have taken two or three times that number to cover our extensive and difficult area. Our numbers grew slowly, never approaching our target, but we moved to larger and better premises near Carlisle Circus. Post 381 or the Cranburn Street Post was destined to become the best known, most efficient post and, unfortunately, the post responsible for one of the most devastated areas of the city. It was this post and its wardens which supplied the background and inspiration on which this record is based.

I have said that the wardens were the Cinderallas of the service. They were the targets for comedians and cartoonists, and the comedy certainly added colour to the drab life of the war years. Unfortunately, a lot of the comedy stuck and the warden became a Keystone Cop type of character. Some of the old jokes are still in circulation and continue to entertain audiences or television viewers.

Admittedly, there were misfits but any voluntary body is bound to attract more than its fair share of characters. Contrary to the false image created, most wardens were a collection of dedicated men and women who were proud of the service. Unlike the other services, the wardens had no special equipment or transport: their strength lay in their own ability. Training covered the basic skills of the other services. The knowledge and performance of these skills was of a high standard, as the wardens would be expected to handle casualties, initiate rescue operations and fight fires while waiting for assistance and, as was seen later, they performed these duties in the face of great danger. In spite of this, the slightly humorous image remained, and sometimes with good cause.

I knew a lot of characters from different posts and they did indeed involve themselves in comical situations. The most ridiculous situations arose when the wardens were given uniforms. It was in the use, or should I say misuse, of the uniform that the characters excelled themselves. There was one fellow who appeared in uniform wearing a bowler hat instead of the regulation beret. One local newspaper carried a cartoon of 'Your Man' but it did not deter him, John continued to wear his bowler hat.

There were others who tended to give the wardens a Dads' Army image, but the prince and the beggar, the fools and the sages all went to make up a great service. I should explain that in civil defence, as a civilian service, we did not salute officers. We did show respect by standing to attention when visiting officers came to our posts. There was one character who persisted in saluting officers irrespective of whether they were in uniform or civilian dress. His routine was to draw himself fully to attention, stamp his foot heavily on the ground, perform a perfect salute and call out in a loud voice 'Sir'. Sammy was never in the army and it is likely that he picked up the routine from some picture he had seen.

I received this treatment on several occasions. I was not an officer but Sammy always regarded me as one and I had to take my share of the saluting with the rest. I can recall vividly one particular occasion. I was standing in the City Hall waiting for the lift to descend. A few other people were also waiting and I was in front. The lift arrived, the doors slid open; there was one occupant poised in the doorway. 'Oh no!', I prayed. 'He won't, not here', I thought, but my prayers were in vain. Sammy spotted me and froze immediately. He pulled himself up to attention right there in the doorway of the lift, nearly put his foot through the floor, gave me his usual masterful salute and his loud 'Sir' echoed through the foyer of the City Hall. Sammy worked in the highway department (now the D.O.E. roads service) and he presented a rare picture as he stood rigidly to attention in the narrow doorway of the lift, attired in clay stained overalls and hob nailed boots. I can still hear the clang of them on the floor of the lift. I was not in uniform but, as I have said, that made no difference to Sam. The whole thing was so comical that although I felt embarrassed, I just had to smile.

The characters always caused some diversion and brightened up the ordinary routine of things. I liked them and found them to be as genuine and conscientious as the rest of us. It was when our training changed to reality that they proved their worth. Sammy was a real godsend with his physical strength, his knowledge of shoring up, and his ability to use a pick and shovel. Many of the other characters acted in a similar manner, showing their mettle when some of those who despised them failed in their duties.

The aim of the wardens was to identify themselves with the community and gain the confidence of the people. However, the nature of our duties in some instances tended to antagonise the public. One big obstacle was the black-out regulations and our insistence on their strict observance. The enforcement of the regulations did not arise from any personal desire to assert our authority over our neighbours. In fact, rigid black-out patrols were mounted at the request of the air ministry. Check flights were made over the city and areas that showed a dangerous breach of the black-out regulations were noted and messages were sent to the district headquarters concerned to have thorough checks. It was explained that even isolated lights could be seen from miles off. This not only presented a danger to our city but could also be used as direction finders by enemy aircraft who had lost their bearings over the Irish Sea or the west coast of England or Scotland.

Another cause for dissension with the locals was the distribution of sandbags. When we first put them outside the houses they were accepted as something novel. The attitude soon changed when the dogs came around and the bags burst and the sand was blown or walked into the houses. When the wardens went to renew them they were told in no uncertain terms to take them away.

We met with the most opposition when we tried to take a census of our neighbourhood. The wardens in working class areas often met with flat refusals to co-operate. The locals were suspicious of anyone asking personal questions or prying into their business as they called it. The suspicion was a hang-over from the depression years when they were subjected to a series of questions about the number in the household. Was the house occupied by one or two families or did they have lodgers? These questions were used by visiting investigators under the hated means test regulations to assess a person's right to benefit.

In order to compile our records we were asking similar questions for a completely different reason. We wished to know how many were in the house and if there were any chronic sick or invalids so that we could give special care and attention in an emergency. Certain illnesses were looked upon as something very personal. They did not discuss handicapped children or chronic illness even with their closest friends. The practice at that time was to hide handicapped children with some sense of shame and they were seldom seen in public. It is all to the good that our attitudes regarding sickness, either mental or physical, are changing. The wardens made many discoveries in all areas when they were attempting to make a census. I am not suggesting that these children or young people were neglected but they were hidden away from the outside world and deprived of the company of friends and neighbours.

The records took the form of a card which we filled in for each family. These cards proved invaluable when the raids came. The cards helped to account for the likely number trapped. They indicated the location of invalids who needed special attention during and after the blitz. We had to work hard to convince the people that the information we wished to collect was for their benefit and would be treated in confidence. We kept at it and our records were reasonably accurate by the time they were needed.

Recruiting and keeping volunteers was a constant battle. It must be understood that service in the civil defence was voluntary. There was no compulsion on a person to remain in the service and so they came and went at will. Some people felt that they should do something in the way of service so they joined the A.R.P. and completed their initial training but lost interest and drifted away. Post 381 was fortunate in that we lost very few recruits. This was the case right through the raids: their dedication and sense of duty never waned.

Although there was no legal obligation to stay with civil defence, those of us who took the work seriously could never understand why anyone left. The wardens' post was the centre of activity in the neighbourhood. A well organized group of wardens knew all that went on in their area and their advice was often sought on many matters outside their normal civil defence duties. At the post there was always something going on. Inter-post darts competitions created a friendly rivalry and an exchange of views with visiting wardens. We had a workshop for handicrafts and model making, open to all our wardens. There were also the usual pastimes, chess, draughts, dominoes and card games. Some posts did not approve of card games but I believed that a man who played a straight game of cards could be trusted to do other things. I don't mean that there was heavy gambling. We had no money for that and I defended my stand on this point on several occasions.

The nine o'clock news on the wireless was the highlight of the day for everyone and at the post it led to a friendly debate of some kind or other. Above all there was always a cup of tea for late callers on their way home. Throughout the dreary years with all the restrictions where could one have found better company and relaxation than at the wardens' post?

There were many posts which did not operate in such an informal way but, as I have said, it was the wardens who made a post. My own personal experiences reinforced my belief that it was the spirit and the comradeship and close ties, not rules and regulations, that held us together and led us to trust in each other and that gave us the strength and resolution to carry out horrible and fearful tasks.

There was a very dangerous opinion circulated in Northern Ireland government circles and within other public bodies. 'The Germans will never come here. They would have to make a 500 mile journey across hostile territory to reach Northern Ireland.' This unfounded and wishful thinking weakened all efforts to interest the public in air raid precautions and led to the ridiculing of those who were interested. It blocked the purchase of equipment especially for the fire, rescue and ambulance services. Cabinet ministers argued that building shelters, the purchase of vehicles and training were a waste of public money. This reference to money haunted the thinking on civil defence from its inception.

The cabinet was divided on air raid precautions. Not until 1940 was a minister for public security appointed, Mr John MacDermott. He was appalled at the state of readiness of the city. When the cabinet finally agreed to the purchase of heavy equipment, supplies were just not available. The shelter programme was in a state of disarray. No Anderson type shelters were available. There were no underground shelters, not due to any fault of the government but due to the nature of the heavy, wet, clay ground on which Belfast was built. Sir James Craig, the Northern Ireland prime minister, in a debate regarding shelters is reported as saying 'Let the people go to the fields and ditches.' There were many more anomalies in the conduct of A.R.P. policy, especially financial haggling with the British government in relation to civil defence expenditure. Thankfully, we volunteers knew little of the squabbling in the cabinet. We had our own feelings about the lack of equipment and public shelters but we carried on with what we had, always hoping for better days.

By 1941 the Germans occupied all the airfields in western Europe and had control of the French coastline and air raids on British cities were launched from these positions. Still the Northern Ireland government felt that Belfast would never have a full scale attack. MacDermott was one of the few who realised the seriousness of the situation but he was still meeting with opposition. He called for evacuation but the public had not been sufficiently instructed as to the danger that threatened the city and they did not take this call seriously.

Belfast was one of the busiest ports in the British Isles. At the deep sea and cross channel berths, important supplies were arriving daily. Ships that could not unload at Liverpool, Glasgow or other British ports were diverted to Belfast. Our engineering and aircraft factories and shipyards were working at full and uninterrupted capacity. Such activity did not escape the notice of the Germans, and yet Belfast was the least defended city in the British Isles.

The defence of Belfast, if it can be called defence, was indeed meagre. There were no searchlights; the squadron had been sent to England. Anti-aircraft batteries consisted of a few heavy guns and light mobile guns. There were no night fighters and the barrage balloon cover was completely inadequate. This, together with an ill equipped and undermanned civil defence and a deplorable shelter policy, was all we had to withstand the fury of the Blitzkrieg.

Our post area was near the docks and part of the industrial belt, and all our training was based on the assumption that the Germans would mount a heavy attack in order to destroy or impede the industrial output and port facilities. The Victoria military barracks right in the heart of our area presented many problems. It divided the post area into four and in our view it made communication very difficult, if not impossible, during an attack. We had to spread our wardens out around the whole barracks complex. The presence of the barracks itself created a hazard. Around the perimeter wall was a densely populated area consisting of small, mill type, back-to-back terraced houses. We always considered the barracks a hazard because we saw a military headquarters as a potential target and in the event of a raid any bombs falling short would crash down on the little houses in the vicinity, causing death and destruction. The situation could have been compared to living at the foot of an active volcano. Everything pointed to a disaster but there was little we could do. Even the shelter facilities in the area were inadequate.

There were, of course, other groups which went to make up the civil defence corps besides the wardens. The fire and ambulance service was known to the public on account of their normal duties but they had no idea of the number of volunteers who waited and trained in the background. It was the volunteer firemen who stood by the side of the full time brigade and fought the fire while the bombs came whistling down. These were the men who risked their lives by going into the dangerous and burning buildings of those who remained trapped.

Likewise, the ambulance crews dashed through the dark and debris littered streets to pick up casualties and render immediate assistance before removing them to the hospital. The first aid crews were mainly volunteers and I can still visualise them as they rushed from site to site and struggled over mountains of debris with loaded stretchers while the city was still under attack.

The rescue service was completely unknown to the public. They were mostly tradesmen connected with the building and construction industry. These were the men who used their skills and equipment to recover those who were trapped or buried under tons of debris. There are many who survived and owe their lives to the skill and courage of these rescue teams. As a warden I must give the rescue men a special mention because the wardens were given a lot of praise that really belonged to them. The rescue men and wardens worked very closely together during the rescue operations, and in many cases it was the wardens who organised the initial rescue work. As wardens we kept close contact with the rescue officers assisting them with our local knowledge. The wardens directed the incoming rescue squads to where people were trapped and the possible number as estimated from our record cards. This close co-operation led people to believe we were all wardens.

The headquarters and communications section was a part of the service completely unknown to the public and even other sections knew little of their procedures. They were responsible for plotting damage and deploying services to the incidents from which they had received reports. The procedure was straightforward. Depots and wardens' posts reported their strength and the number of vehicles available. Operations staff marked up the strength reports on resources boards and marked or pinned on large wall maps the sites and nature of damage as reports came through from police or wardens. District control centres also sent situation reports to central control who were then in a position to compile an overall picture of what was happening throughout the city.

This was the text book plan, simple and operational. The warden's duty was to report damage and the estimated number of casualties. District control, knowing what services were available, would order the despatch of appropriate services or ask central control for help. However, everything that could go wrong often went wrong. There were not sufficient services. In the early part of the night of a raid, the situation maps in the damaged areas became a forest of coloured pins and the resources boards were cleared. For those responsible for the control of the specialist services it must have been a heart-breaking sight. The greatest upset was the complete disruption of communications. During the worst raid, Belfast was completely isolated from the rest of the United Kingdom.

Wardens risked their lives carrying their messages by hand, in some cases over a mile, through debris and past burning buildings while the planes above continued to drop their deadly cargo. As the night went on and the situation grew worse we knew we were no longer going to hear the clang of a fire engine or the roar of a heavy rescue vehicle or ambulance coming in response to our messages.

The final and very important section was welfare. Their preparations were based on estimates but no planning could have forseen the extent of the destruction, the panic, or the demand that was to be put on this voluntary service. They were in theory responsible for rest centres, homeless people, emergency feeding, evacuation and documentation. When called upon they handled these duties plus all the other human problems that arose in the wake of the greatest disaster ever experienced in the history of our city.

The A.R.P. in Belfast was divided into civil defence districts. These were known by letters: A was the city centre; B, West Belfast, Falls Road and Shankill; C covered the Crumlin Road and Oldpark area; D covered the Antrim Road and Carlisle Circus; E was responsible for the whole east side of the city; F was the south side, Lisburn Road and Ormeau Road; G was York Street, York Road and the dockland area; H was the harbour estate and had its own services.

Each district had its own auxiliary fire service (A.F.S.), rescue, first aid and ambulance depots, control centre and a number of wardens' posts scattered throughout the area. Rural areas were organised to offer assistance to Belfast or Londonderry in the case of an emergency.

This was the plan of operations, and the people who volunteered to carry it out were ordinary men and women who did their daily work and attended to their families. The diversity of the tasks undertaken was tremendous and in spite of their training and planning they were not mentally prepared for the horrible sights they were to encounter. It is to their credit that they helped to nurse a battered and demoralised city back to normality.

2   The raids begin: the tour of the ports

The opening months of 1941 saw the start of a new plan in German bombing tactics. Instead of concentrating fully on London they turned their attention to other British cities. A definite plan soon emerged from this new strategy and was referred to as the tour of the ports in some circles. During this period Hull, Portsmouth, Swansea, Cardiff, Liverpool and Merseyside, and Glasgow and Clydeside were heavily bombed.

A glance at a map of Great Britain will show that the Germans had embarked on a systematic plan of bombing around the coast, hitting at the most important ports in an attempt to destroy or paralyse our shipping facilities.

Belfast was included in this German plan to destroy British ports and was, according to one of the pilots who took part in the great fire attack on the city on 4th May, a specially selected target. In a broadcast from Berlin the pilot said that Belfast had enjoyed immunity from air raids. Her industrial and port facilities were adding considerably to the British war effort. This situation could no longer be tolerated and an operation was ordered to destroy the port and the industrial parts of the city.

When the German Luftwaffe attacked the city it was apparent from the number of planes taking part, and the type of weapons used, that the city had indeed been singled out for special attention. It was estimated that over 200 planes took part in the major raids and, in the early years of the war, to stage such a long distance air raid suggested the importance which the Germans placed on it.

Belfast experienced her first air attacks in early April 1941. Reporting of the raids was scanty. Newspapers carried only brief official statements in headline form: *Enemy aircraft in action over N. Ireland. The attack was of short duration. Damage and casualties were slight.* The first raid hit the railway complex at York Road and a few houses fronting the main road were damaged. The next raid was on 7th April and was centred on East Belfast, the shipyard and aircraft factory.

Although the raids were of short duration they meant a full alert as far as the A.R.P. operations were concerned. On the sound of the sirens, civil defence personnel reported to their respective posts and depots.

On the occasion of the first night alert on 7th April, an air of excitement filled the duty room as volunteers hurried in to report for duty. Amid the excitement and the general tension in every post and depot throughout the city we all had our own private thoughts about what would happen during the night to come.

I left the post with a group of my wardens. As I had been appointed senior warden for our section, I was responsible for the posting and briefing of the wardens in my sector. The men knew the area they were to patrol and when they had all been deployed I continued my patrol along down Clifton Street to the corner of North Queen Street where I made contact with a Constable Foster. This was one of our official points of contact with the police and was also at that time the boundary of two police districts (D and G) and three post areas. I stood in conversation with the policeman for a short time and told him of our arrangements for covering the area and the number of men available over the whole patch. I took my leave of him, said I would be back shortly and continued my patrol along North Queen Street where I met up with some wardens who were making their way down from the upper post area. This was the plan we had worked out to enable us to cover the whole area and to keep contact with our own wardens and those of the adjoining posts. As I have explained, Victoria military barracks was right in the heart of our area, and cut it into four sections. Apart from the inconvenience of patrolling we had other forebodings which, unfortunately, turned out to be correct.

After a brief conversation with the wardens I returned to Clifton Street and they went up New Lodge Road, which was the only point of entry into the heart of the area after leaving Clifton Street. On my return I found that my companion had been joined by two other policemen. As I approached, I could hear the language of the newcomers was rather coarse. In fact four letter words seemed to make up a good part of their vocabulary. Foster was a religious man and he did not approve of the conversation. I always put the over use of swear words down to tension. 'I think we should take a walk around, lad, and see what is happening,' he said. We crossed the road and took up a new position in the doorway of Murray's public house which was then situated at the corner of Clifton Street and Upper Library Street (Carrick Hill). The door was on the junction of the two streets which met in a sharp point. It was a good vantage point and we could see faintly in all directions in the darkness.

When we had settled ourselves he said 'I don't like that language at any time but at a time like this it is downright blasphemy.' I liked his attitude; he seemed to me to be the right kind of fellow and I was pleased that we saw eye to eye on such an occasion. I mention this incident because I was convinced that we could all carry out our duties better when working with those whom we trusted. I was happy that I had some confidence in this stranger. Tonight's operation was not an exercise but a real encounter with the enemy in which lives could be at stake.

We chatted comfortably. He told me some of his experiences and I added some comical situations that arose at work. There was no sign of enemy activity but there was an uncanny silence that was frightening. We listened intently from time to time. The city centre was close by but there was no sound of any kind. I recalled the lines of a poem which spoke of a silence one could almost hear.

From time to time I scanned the dark sky above. There were no searchlights and still that awful silence seemed to haunt us. Suddenly there was the sound of an explosion some distance away. It was either a freak blast wave or a bomb of some magnitude which threw us against the bar door and we could hear bottles and glasses come tumbling down inside. The blast took us by surprise. We had been treating the night with some indifference as we stood joking and chatting. The violent

explosion jerked us into a more serious mood as we stood
straining our ears in an effort to pick up the sound of planes
which we expected to break out of the clouds at any moment.

Since we had crossed the road from our meeting point I
realised that if any of my wardens were looking for me they
would not see me in the darkness so we returned to our
original position and continued to listen and scan the sky.
Contact with the other wardens was more important now that
enemy planes were in action over the city. I decided to go and
get a report on the state of the area. The constable said he
would go with me. I suppose he felt uncomfortable being left
alone or maybe he had no desire to meet up with his other
comrades who were still in the area.

The silence still hung over the neighbourhood and we were
the only moving things to be seen. The blackout was complete,
not a chink of light showing. It was like looking out in the
darkness over a vast ocean.

From somewhere in the stillness of the night a babble of
conversation came floating towards us. The sound was like
music to my ears and soon two wardens emerged from the
darkness. They had already made contact with some others
from the post and they were a mine of information. According
to them, Crumlin Road, Carlisle Circus, Antrim Road, New
Lodge Road and Duncairn Gardens were clear; there was no
damage so far. We completed the report by confirming that the
area stretching back to the city centre was also clear. It
appeared that enemy activity was still confined to East
Belfast.

We went back towards Clifton Street and listened to the
footsteps of my comrades as they faded in the darkness. It
looked as if the raid was not going to develop and we felt more
at ease as we walked along. Foster remarked on how the
wardens kept contact with each other and passed on messages. I explained that the wardens had no transport or means
of communication and that in the event of an attack all movement and transmission of messages would have to be done on
foot. I explained further that we did a lot of training with this in
view, and that most wardens knew their areas thoroughly,
including back alley ways and alternate routes, in and out, in
the event of roads being blocked by debris or unexploded

bombs. 'Not bad at all for a bunch of amateurs,' he said with a laugh.

'Amateurs maybe,' I replied, 'but I'll bet you've met some of the best professionals tonight. Those blokes are part of a squad that would amaze you if you heard their plans for going into action.'

I knew he thought I was making fun but the truth of those words was certainly put to the test at a later date. While we were engaged in this light conversation the dreadful silence was broken by the steady wailing note of the sirens. The sound of the 'all clear' had a magic all its own and only those who have experienced it can fully appreciate what it meant to a frightened populace. To the wardens as they wandered about the darkened streets it brought a feeling of deep relief because not only did they have their own safety to think of but also the ever present feeling of responsibility for the safety of their neighbourhood.

East Belfast was the target for the raid that night and although it had, in the words of the official statement, been of short duration, it did result in some deaths. Among those who died were five firewatchers and a fireman.

Legislation introduced in 1940 made it compulsory for owners of industrial and commercial premises to have them patrolled at night in order to give an early warning in the case of fire or the opportunity to tackle incendiary bombs before they fully ignited and caused major fires. Firewatchers, as these guards were known, were recruited from the employees on a rota basis. They received no remuneration for their night's duty except a meal allowance of three shillings (15p). No one seemed to give much attention to the dangers to which the firewatcher were exposed and it is significant that many lost their lives in the ensuing raids.

I made my way back to the post. Some wardens were already there and others came hurrying in from their patrols. We were all very excited and eager to tell our stories and make our reports. There was no damage in the post area and, according to procedure, a no damage report was sent to district headquarters. We stood about exchanging experiences while we waited for stand down orders or a request for help from some other post area. Eventually stand down orders came through and we went home somewhat excited but very thoughtful. It had been our first night alert. We had been lucky to receive our baptism without fire.

Several important lessons and warning messages came out of the experience. The tension was something new. It could not be simulated by exercises – nor could alertness or keen observation and quick decision making. We realised from our constant patrolling just how difficult and dangerous communication and control would be if the city came under a heavy attack.

For myself I was convinced that fate played a part in the circumstances which caused me to cross the road that night to a point where I was hit by a freak blast wave. I discovered next day it was a parachute mine which fell in the shipyard complex. I was so much impressed by the incident that on another occasion the memory triggered off an immediate response which saved my life and that of a companion.

The raid alerted all concerned with the safety of the city. Intelligence reports indicated the serious possibility of a major threat to the city. Finance had played a big part in the neglect of air raid precautions for Belfast and other parts of the province. Too much had been left undone. Our shelter programme was far behind schedule. Equipment for civil defence especially fire, rescue and ambulance was in no way on par with the importance of Belfast's role in the war effort or the growing threat to the city. Those who were responsible for the defence of the city did not realise when they spoke of the waste of public money, that civil defence was the only defence we would have against the bombs, mines and incendiaries.

Unfortunately, time was running out and there remained but one week to prepare for the greatest disaster in the history of our city. The authorities could only wait and hope. When disaster struck it was the civil defence volunteers who were faced with the unenviable task of picking up the pieces.

3   The Easter blitz, 1941

Easter Tuesday 1941 was a beautiful day and as I passed through the city I noted the carefree holiday spirit even amongst those who were unable to go away on a proper holiday. Queues of people, mostly families, were waiting for tramcars. Bellevue and Greencastle were the venues favoured by the crowd. Children carrying baskets of sandwiches and refreshments danced about and shouted excitedly as tramcars lumbered up noisily to the loading point.

At that moment no one could have imagined what a difference a few hours would make. Perhaps for some of those children it was to be their last picnic.

I called into the post on my way home and saw a complete contrast to the happy, carefree atmosphere that I had just left. The wardens were already on alert. Reports of enemy reconnaissance aircraft over the city had been confirmed by headquarters. No alert was sounded but there were reports of gunfire in some areas and the barrage balloons were sent up. I liked to see the barrage balloons. They always looked so graceful as they floated and bobbed about at the end of their cables. They held a memory for me far removed from war with all its horrors. The sight of them often brought me back to the time as a young boy when I had stood and watched the great Zeppelin R 101 as it passed over Belfast in 1930.

The reconnaissance aircraft caused us some concern. A number of our wardens were away on holiday and if anything serious were to happen we would find ourselves severely undermanned, as even with a full turnout our strength, like other posts, was low. A muster of available wardens was made and we held ourselves in readiness for the rest of the day. Stirrup pumps were tested, stretchers and blankets were made ready for use, first aid kits and water bottles were filled and a few axes and crowbars completed our equipment. We borrowed extra buckets from our own homes and sent out patrols that evening to check on how many people were still away on holidays and also to take a note of empty premises.

The day remained tense, but we kept busy, trying to forsee every eventuality. We filled sandbags and practised writing out damage reports. It seemed crazy that we were spending Easter Tuesday this way when others were out and about enjoying themselves, but there was a war on. Elsewhere the holiday spirit was still apparent as night approached and the streets were thronged with returning holidaymakers, many of them returning to death or terrible injuries or a lifetime of unforgettable memories.

At 10.45 p.m. the wailing sirens gave warning that enemy aircraft were approaching the city. The wardens who had stood by during the day were already at the post; others came hurrying in to report for duty. Even those who had been on holiday and had scarcely time to unpack, reported for duty. Post 381 turned out at full strength. It was a good sign of the spirit that had become part of the post. This was the spirit that sustained them throughout the night and made heroes out of ordinary men.

After a short briefing by our group warden, each senior warden checked with his own team of men and led them out. My section numbered about seven or eight men. They knew their positions and as they moved along they dropped out in twos until we were scattered throughout the entire area, lonely and isolated as we patrolled the dark, deserted streets. Again, it was my duty to cover the whole sector and to keep in contact with as many wardens as possible. The wardens knew the drill and the points where I would try and make contact with them.

Soon the plan of action fell into place throughout the city. The wardens were on the streets acting as the eyes of the civil defence corps. The firemen, rescue and ambulance service personnel were standing by at their depots. These services would be called out on receipt of a message from district control based on reports of damage coming from wardens or police.

My wardens had taken up their positions and I was now alone as I made by way down Clifton Street. The route was lined with a number of old oil drums. They were part of a defence scheme which we called smoke screens, the purpose being to blur the outlines of the buildings. Soldiers from the nearby barracks set them alight when the sirens were sounded and they were belching forth a heavy black cloud of evil smelling smoke which enveloped the area like a thick fog. My companion that night at the contact point was police constable Hall who was an elderly man and the smoke sent him into several severe bouts of coughing. The smoke did not affect my breathing but it attacked my eyes and I could feel them burning. There was no escape from it as the barrels were spread out along the perimeter of the barracks and as the smoke built up it became extremely uncomfortable.

Suddenly the city was illuminated by giant flares which floated down on parachutes. How can I find words to describe the intensity of the brilliance which tore through the darkness and bathed the city in a light greater than the sun at noon? Every building stood out in detail and we could see in all directions. Royal Avenue, North Street and Carlisle Circus were plainly visible whereas a few seconds previously one could scarcely see an outstretched hand. The flares hung like giant electric lamps up in the sky. The flares themselves did not offer any threat to us but as we stood in the open bathed in their white light it was a disturbing and frightening experience. Frightening, because the city was exposed to the planes which could be hovering above like giant vultures waiting to dive on their prey. As I stood in the now fading light of the flares the thought came to me. Were the blackout, the smoke screens and hooded car lights of any use? At that moment it appeared to me that they were all totally ineffective. The build-up to the raid suggested a heavy attack and I could not help thinking that tonight Belfast was about to experience the full horror of war.

CITY AND COUNTY BOROUGH OF BELFAST

AIR RAID PRECAUTIONS

THIS IS TO CERTIFY that..............................

James Doherty,

8 Cranburn Street.

has been duly appointed as an Air Raid Warden. This is his authority to carry out the duties laid upon Wardens by the County Borough of Belfast.

Signed..

Major.
Air Raid Precautions Officer.

Date of Issue......11th June, 1940.

Signature of Warden :

The author's pass.

4   The raid develops

The flares burned out and the city returned to darkness. We had almost forgotten about the smoke but it had been there all the time we had stood transfixed. The flares had only penetrated but did not disperse the smoke and now the fumes seemed more noxious than before.

There was not much time to concern ourselves about the unpleasantness of the smoke. The sudden roar of planes as they came thundering and dropping from the sky shook us into action. For the purpose of contact and relay of messages our duty point was excellent but it lacked cover of any description. At that moment we were right out in the open. Enemy aircraft were directly overhead and the only likely target was the barracks which was only some yards from where we were standing. Our only protection was to get down close to the low spiked wall that surrounded the old people's home just behind us, Clifton House. The planes flew overhead in relays and started bombing. In our cramped position we could hear the explosions and feel the vibrations and the ground below us shook as the planes discharged their deadly cargoes. Added to the growing tumult of noise was the constant barrage put up by the gunners in the barracks. They were firing blindly in an attempt to keep the raiders away. Then there was a sudden silence; the guns went quiet but the planes continued to pound their target.

The barracks, as I have said, covered an appreciable area with living quarters, stores, administration blocks and a multitude of other buildings. The bombers seemed set on the complete destruction of the barracks and the planes returned again and again throughout the night bombing and blasting, and, unfortunately, as we had feared, the little houses around the barracks also suffered tremendous damage and the death toll rose steadily during the night.

With the exception of the drone of the heavily laden planes everything fell silent again. Our position offered little protection even from falling shrapnel which we could hear dropping around us. We decided, however, to remain where we were, in case we ran into trouble while attempting to move to a more sheltered position. At the height of the attack we were tempted to make a bolt for better cover.

However, although we were in danger from a direct blast, at least we would not be trapped under piles of debris, so we stayed where we were.

The attack lasted, perhaps, only about five minutes but as we sheltered on the ground it seemed as if it would never end. We listened intently as the planes moved on in search of new targets. The silence returned; everything was the same as before and the smoke screens were still belching out their smoke. There was no one else in the area but ourselves. We got up from our cramped position and moved about to relieve our aching muscles, still listening and watching for the return of the planes.

I had not received any damage reports but I was anxious about the other wardens operating in the area and the streets in their charge and I decided to try and contact them. The constable came along with me and we made our way along North Queen Street. As far as we could see everything was all right from the civilian point of view. As far as the barracks was concerned, the military would attend to their damage and would not call on the civil authorities.

Apart from the barracks, I believed that some damage must have occurred in the Antrim Road or New Lodge Road areas. We were isolated from the rest of our patch so I could only speculate on the overall position. I decided to return to our original position and make my way back to the post via Carlisle Circus. We returned to Clifton Street and as we stood there for a few minutes before leaving, we heard the sound of young voices drifting towards us from somewhere down Donegall Street and as they drew closer we could hear their excited laughter. I recognised them as they emerged in the darkness. They were a group of wardens from the Trinity Street post just across the road. There had been a well attended Irish night of song and dance in the Ulster Hall and my young friends had been at it. When the sirens sounded the well-known singer and star of the show, Delia Murphy, appealed to the crowd to remain in the hall and she led them in a community sing-song. It was thought that the alert would only be a short one as on previous occasions. The function was well attended and the hall was packed to capacity. People had come from all over the city and they joined in the singing which lasted the entire night until the all clear sounded. It is believed that many lives were saved by this unprecedented marathon sing-song.

The young wardens, however, had decided that it was their duty to report to their post. They left the hall and made their way through the town still in a happy and excited mood in spite of the alert. They wished us good-night and I suggested we would meet later. They crossed the road singing a song which they had probably heard earlier in the night at the concert. We listened as their happy voices faded as they disappeared in the darkness. In a few minutes they and other companions at the Trinity Street post were dead, killed by a parachute mine which I narrowly escaped.

There was no sign of enemy activity so I took the opportunity to make tour and report to the post. The constable said he would go to his station which was in the same direction that I intended to go. We moved off and luckily for us the constable was looking towards the sky. 'What's that, lad?' he asked as he tugged at my sleeve and pointed upwards. I did not take time to look in the direction of the pointing finger. I knew what it was. The memory of the first exploding parachute mine was still fresh. I shouted 'Down' and at the same time I pushed him to the ground and threw myself alongside him.

Time seemed to stop during the few seconds we lay on the ground waiting as the mine came swishing through the air towards us. Our future, as Winston Churchill put it, when he condemned the use of parachute mines, depended on a gust of wind. What seemed like a thousand years was, in fact, only seconds. The mine did not reach the ground but struck the spire of the Trinity Street Church and exploded immediately.

The whole world seemed to rock; slates, bricks, earth and

flying glass rained down on us. I dug my face well down into my folded arms for protection and lay there for what seemed an eternity. I could hear debris still falling but not with the same force. Dust was forced into my nostrils and mouth and I could scarcely breathe. But by a miracle we were alive.

We were caught in the blast of a parachute mine which had reduced a granite-built church to rubble and devastated the surrounding area. I could scarcely believe that we had survived. We picked ourselves up and looked around. The air was still thick with dust which mingled with the smoke and made breathing uncomfortable. We did not speak but just stood trembling and breathing heavily. We had been through a frightening experience within the previous few minutes and were naturally suffering from shock. I seem to remember saying 'Jerry nearly got us there,' trying to make light of the situation.

In spite of his age, the constable was a hardy old veteran and was already showing signs of recovery. I noticed that his hand was bleeding. He had been hit by a piece of flying glass or other brick-bat. I took a bandage from my kit and as I applied it to the wound I felt a hint of a smile. The thought had struck me that after two years of war this was my first casualty. He started back to his station and I walked up Clifton Street with him. At Glenravel Street he thanked me, shook my hand and we parted. I wondered then and I have often wondered since, what would have happened had he not noticed that parachute as we walked along together.

I saw him safely back to his station. It was frightening to be alone on such a night and in such circumstances, but I felt that I had to go back and do something. Even alone, there might be something I could do. Somewhere in that maze of rubble there had to be someone who needed help.

I stumbled and slipped in the debris as I moved about in the darkness. I had my torch but I did not use it. Perhaps the theory of the black-out was getting through to me: even small lights can be seen at a distance. Although I knew the district well I found it difficult to find my bearings. A piece of instruction came to me which up to that time had been meaningless. I remembered an instructor warning that when landmarks disappeared it would be very hard to find one's way around a damaged area. However, it was clear to me that the Trinity Street post was no more.

As the extent of the damage became clearer to me, I realised that it was useless to continue as I had been doing. I was just moving about in circles. I took up a position at what I considered was a good vantage point. The debris here was thinner and I was able to move about with more freedom. I kept within this area and moved around, shouting to see if anyone was there. I continued to call out and listened but all I heard was my own voice echoing back. I moved further in and called again. This time I heard voices and I was overjoyed when people came staggering towards me. They were confused and had been wandering in the debris. I tried to reassure them and told them that I would bring them out to the road. I called out again and invited them to join me. We kept on shouting as we moved out. More voices answered us and I shouted 'Over here, over here!' The satisfaction of finding people alive buoyed me up. My own terrifying experience of a few minutes ago was forgotten. It was a feeling that I have never forgotten, being able to help someone in need. They were all in a state of shock. One man had twisted or broken his ankle. I stayed with him and helped him along. Near Clifton Street another group of people joined us. A woman in this group had severe facial injuries. Like the others, they were wandering about lost in the maze of debris and shock had left them with no recollection of what had happened to them or how they had got there. There were many similar cases with the same pattern. Those civil defence workers who found casualties wandering about could illicit no information from them and when they handed them over to first aid posts or hospitals, they could only give the location of where they found them as a key to their identity.

I had now nine people to care for and I brought them through the debris strewn streets into Clifton Street and across the road to a shelter in Frederick Street. The woman required medical treatment. There was little I could do for her so I decided that I would have to leave them and go for help. The man too needed attention to his ankle. They did not want me to leave them. I think that in their shocked state they associated me with their safety and felt that if I left them something terrible would happen. I did my best to convince them that I had to go and told them not to leave the shelter until I came back. When I shone my torch around I found a few other people in the shelter. They were huddled in the far corner. They too, were frightened but not hurt. They had sought shelter when the sirens had sounded. I asked them to watch the other people for me until I returned. I hoped that looking after someone else would help them in their own fear. Having satisfied myself that I had done all I could, I went out in search of help.

There was a large first aid and ambulance depot in Academy Street a few hundred yards away off York Street and I made my way down to it. Fires were burning fiercely in the city centre and I could hear heavy explosions in the High Street direction. I made my report and asked them to pass the terrible news about the wardens' post in Trinity Street to my control centre in D District. A first aid team and transport came back with me. I pointed out what I considered to be the most serious cases and told them I would have to go. I learned later that the lady with the facial injury had to have an eye removed.

I went in once more to Trinity Street but in the darkness I could locate no more casualties. I consoled myself that all the wardens could not have been killed in the disaster. There must have been some on patrol in another part of the area when the mine struck. The rescue and ambulance services would soon be at the scene and with the help of the local wardens a proper operation would be mounted. The post itself was crushed beneath tons of masonry which came cascading down on it when the massive spire of the church collapsed. For those who lay beneath the dark pile of granite it was the end of the road. I paused for a few more moments in silent prayer before setting off for my own post.

Carlisle Circus and the Antrim Road showed signs of a heavy attack and my street was a shambles. What had been a row of neat terrace houses was now a mountain of rubble. I stood gazing at the mound which was once my home. I was dazed and frightened, thinking about my family, my father, my mother and sister. Less than an hour previously I had marvelled at my own miraculous escape. I was alive, I thought, but now my own life did not hold the same value for me. When I had spoken to them about taking shelter they often said that they would prefer to stay in the house rather than go to the shelters.

Our shelters were far from being suitable places to spend a night. Doors were never fitted to them and they had lain neglected since they were built. Local residents used them as places for dumping rubbish and throughout the city they were often used as public conveniences. Overall they were dark, evil smelling, airless dungeons. Knowing the general feeling with which the public regarded the shelters only increased my panic. In a daze I made my way to the post, almost afraid to hear the news I so much wanted to know. I met some wardens who assured me that my family were safe. When the attack started in the barrack's area, the wardens went around and advised the residents to go to the shelters, as the area was so dangerous. I thanked them but words were inadequate to express my deep sense of relief and gratitude.

I was personally overjoyed and thankful that the wardens had acted promptly and put our plan in relation to the barracks into operation. Our prediction, which likened people living at the foot of an active volcano to our own situation, was coming true. Thousands, however, throughout the city did not go to the shelters and, unfortunately, many perished that night.

At the post I told them about the Trinity Street disaster and the news was received with horror. The staff at Trinity Street post were our close friends. We served the same community and personal friendships had developed between the wardens of the two posts. Telephone communication was disrupted and this was the first information they had about anything outside our own area. I told them about the fires in the city centre and York Street that I had seen earlier. They listened intently; so far there had been no reports of fire in our post area.

I said I would go to the shelter and let my family know that I was safe. It is strange how quickly one's thoughts can change. A few minutes earlier I was anxious about my family and now my thoughts were that they would be anxious about me. I made my way to the shelter and went in. The scene was pathetic. There were about sixty people huddled together. Some were sitting on the ground, others were standing.

Children were crying with fear. They did not understand why they were there. I used my torch to look around. I called out and my sister Veronica answered me. After the moments of anguish which gripped me as I stood beside the heap of twisted masonry that had been my home, the joy of being reunited with my family was beyond all bounds of human expression. I did not disturb them by telling them my experiences or how bad it was outside. They did not know that our home and all our neighbours' houses were destroyed. The other people were glad to see me. They were my neighbours and they had shared my family's anxiety.

They all had their families with them and I had been the only one who was missing. Some of them were thirsty and I shared my water bottle with them as best I could and promised to bring some more as soon as I could. The children were nervous and unsettled. I knew them all and we got on well together. I had often put my haversack over their shoulders and let them wear my helmet. They loved this dressing up and I was very popular with the kids in the area. I spent a few more minutes with them but there was lots of work for me to do outside so I returned to the post.

Back at the post there was a feeling of gloom and despair. Messages requesting help had been sent to control but none of our wardens on patrol had reported any services arriving. Even as we spoke we could hear the continuous thunder of bombs exploding. The droning sound of the heavy bombers could be heard overhead as they flew over the city without any opposition. We were defenceless against the onslaught. Telephone communication was disrupted and our only means of contact was on foot. Wardens on patrol did their best to let the post know what was happening. Everywhere there was the problem of having no means of getting fast and reliable information.

Every post had some young cyclists who were known as the messenger service. In training exercises the system worked well and the transmission of messages went without a hitch. But in actual raids such as we were experiencing their use even to take an urgent message was a responsibility that few in charge would have relished. When I see young people today playing about with C.B. radios and note how clear and uninterrupted their transmissions are, I often think, 'What would we have given for such a system?'

I went out with one of my companions to see the situation for myself and to bring back a report of damage and casualties. As we walked around we met one of the local shopkeepers and after a brief conversation he invited us into his shop and gave us some minerals, sweets and biscuits for the children. Back at the post we collected a large can of water, some cups and a few candles and went back down to the large shelter. A comical thought struck me. I would organise a picnic for the kids. It would indeed be the strangest picnic ever. Instead of an Easter picnic at the seaside, it was in a dark shelter at the height of a blitz. The idea was crazy but I liked it. I told the parents the children would love it and that it would help to settle them. At any rate, as we left I could feel a happier atmosphere about the place. Even the candles made a difference. The people who previously were huddled together in fear were now showing a new spirit.

Pleas for help were piling up at the post and we realised that little help could be expected. The text book instruction on how to summon help was not going to work under the circumstances prevailing at the time. The fury and weight of the attack had soon put the services in difficulties. The fire, rescue and ambulance services were under pressure and they just could not cope with the terrific build up of fires, damage and casualties. They did not have the resources to meet such an onslaught.

We as wardens, a mere handful of men and boys, were left with an impossible responsibility. Each and everyone of us would have to act as rescuer, doctor, fireman and counsellor. The saving of life was all that mattered now. If only one life could be saved in the midst of all the destruction then something would have been achieved. As we considered our situation, the drone of the heavy planes above and continued explosions reminded us that further death and destruction was still to come. The more active of us decided to form a type of flying squad to investigate the various sites of damage and do what we could for the injured or partially trapped. So it was that a handful of wardens were the only defence and help the entire neighbourhood could expect. Only God and ourselves

know how we managed to get through that night and the
following days. We left the post carrying our equipment which
was crude but effective. It consisted of a few pick-axes, crowbars, some stretchers, hand axes and a few stirrup pumps and
buckets. We could have done with some transport but we were
not an affluent group and there was not a car owner among us.
We divided the equipment and went out on the grim and
dangerous task. Our plan was simple; we would move from
site to site, treat the wounded, effect any possible rescue with
our picks and crowbars and attack any fires which we though
we could control. It was a hit and run operation but we hoped
to achieve something in what appeared to be a hopeless
situation.

Lincoln Avenue was the first site we tackled. Damage resulting from a parachute mine was severe and 15 people were
killed in this single incident and a large crater was left. In such
cases we did not expect to find anyone alive. Nevertheless, we
started to search the debris for any signs of life. Warden John
Montague and myself started to search around the crater itself.
We had only the dim light from our hooded lamps. I was
working into the mouth of the crater when I thought I heard a
movement at the bottom. I called John and we climbed down
into the crater and started to clear a heap of debris and timber
from where I thought I had heard the noise. To our delight we
found two people. They did not appear to be injured and we
were able to get them out with the assistance of some of the
other wardens who came down in answer to our calls. I knew
the Duffy family and the the young man whom we had found
was a classmate of mine and the same age. We found the rest of
the family later. They were all dead, blown to pieces as were
the rest of the victims of the explosion. It was one of those
strange happenings in life. The Duffy family did not live in the
district originally but had come to live there in recent years. I
never saw them again but they left me an unsolved riddle.
How did these people come to be at the bottom of the crater?
They could not have fallen in because they were buried under
a heap of timber and debris. Could they possibly have been
lifted by the blast and thrown into the crater uninjured? It
is a question that I have asked myself many times, but the
mystery remains. I have spoken to others who were lucky to

survive but they can give no account of their miraculous escapes.

Our success gave us great encouragement and we set off again. This time we went to the Annadale Street area, a scene of terrible destruction and carnage. It must be understood that weapons used on this built-up area were intended for use on the shipyard, aircraft factories and industrial complexes. One of these bombs was sufficient to reduce streets of little back-to-back houses to mountains of rubble. At this site we met with what must be the most discouraging part of rescue work. Fire had broken out in the debris. This was one of the incidents that will live for ever in my memory. The manner in which heavy timbers, doors and beams were protruding from the debris suggested that we might find some bodies alive in voids (air spaces) down in the rubble. However, the smoldering fires made rescue attempts very difficult. Nevertheless, we tackled the pile of masonry with picks and iron bars. We pulled at heavy debris with our bare hands and gently moved large beams aside. A passing auxiliary fire service team with a trailer pump sprayed the hot bricks to cool them as we dug feverishly to reach the bodies which we believed were there. When we eventually came across some bodies they had been cooked under the hot bricks. What a sight it was. In a normal rescue operation many victims were removed injured but alive from similar debris. But in situations such as I have described we could only expect horror. Even as I write I find it difficult to describe the full ghastliness of the scene.

All around us was death. Burke Street had disappeared; not a house was standing. The death toll here was high, as it was in this entire area. Everywhere we went we met with death and the horror of it all was that the dead outnumbered the injured.

I knew these people well and I had often chatted with them as I passed through the streets on patrol and the children would share their sweets or walk along with me. Now it was heartbreaking to think of their mangled bodies below those mounds of rubble. This was the hardest part of the warden's job. He was part of the community. The other services did not have this previous personal contact with the victims.

We moved on into the heart of the area. Here we met once more with bomb damage, fires and hysterical residents. Water and sewage from fractured mains flooded the streets. In some places gas mains were burning fiercely and people were terrified that they would explode or that the flames would travel into their houses and set them on fire. We did not have much knowledge of this kind of damage, but we understood that the best thing to do was to let them burn and not to try and put them out. Everywhere terrified residents pleaded with us to stay with them. We advised them to go to the shelters where at least they would be safer than in their little houses. In some cases we went with them and stayed for a while with them. I think shelters were the most depressing places I visited that night, and we felt sorry for those distressed people who had to seek comfort within those damp, dark dungeons. But we had to move on, the saving of a life or extinguishing a fire depended on our being on the spot quickly. We assured them that we would be back and continued on our way. We met with other patrolling wardens who were glad of our company. I have tried to explain the loneliness of the night for those who were on patrol, watching, reporting and by their very presence helping to relieve the fears of the residents.

After seeing those poor wretches cowering like frightened animals, we agreed to drop into shelters from time to time to let those inside know that the wardens were nearby. It was good that we did so because we found two cases of women in labour. This was something quite new to us but we were able to get help as our local knowledge included the names of women, not qualified midwives, but people who could handle this kind of emergency. In the mill community there were many housewives who had attended at scores of births and the local people trusted and depended on them. We were able to locate a few of these 'handy women' as they were known and I believe it is worthy of record that without any hesitation they left the safety of their shelter and came with us, forgetting the danger of the night for the sake of others.

Time passed very slowly, there was no let up in the havoc being wrought by the bombers. They just seemed to be patrolling our streets and the continuous drone was frightening. Where would the bombs fall next? Was there no defence for the city? Would we all be dead before the night was through? Somewhere in the docks area we heard the sound of heavy gunfire and the sky was ablaze with bursting shells and tracer bullets. It was a refreshing sight. I think it was Churchill who said during the London raids 'Let the guns keep firing: it's good for the morale of the people.' The firing came from a naval vessel the *Furious*; apparently there were other armed merchant ships in the docks that night but owing to the complete breakdown of communications no instructions for a barrage were given.

About this time one of the patrolling wardens reported a terrible disaster at the York Street mill. The mill was not officially in our district but was just across the road on the boundary line and came under G District administration. Our squad was only a few hundred yards from the disaster and we made off towards it. The scene was indescribable. A direct hit on the mill caused a large section about sixty yards long to come down like an avalanche on two little streets, Vere Street and Sussex Street, which nestled in the shadows of the towering factory. The death toll was high. The small mill houses crumbled under the weight of the fallen masonry. Small shelters in the street also crumbled, killing those inside. Thirty-nine people were killed and many were seriously injured in this incident. I thought, as we gazed at the mass of twisted girders and concrete, that we were witnessing the death of a community and a way of life.

There were some wardens from Great Georges Street post already there and we joined them. Experience of the night had taught us that casualties were to be found everywhere around an incident. We made our way down Earl Street and approached the damage from that side. The lower section of Vere Street was not so badly damaged, the upper end of the street had taken the full weight of the disaster. People were wandering about aimlessly, staring at their shattered homes. Some were crying. It was a closely knit community and those who died were close lifelong friends or relatives. Many remained huddled together in the ruins of their houses, afraid to come out. We could only speak to them and explain that they were safe now, that they had escaped the explosion, and that soon it would be all over. The local wardens were successful in rescuing some people where the mass of debris was lighter. We joined them and attended to casualties. Our presence was a bit of a boost to the hard pressed wardens. Like ourselves they were undermanned and their area, like our own, was heavily damaged. Soon we were off again on what appeared to be a never ending ordeal.

The mill people were well known to me. As a youngster I often sat terrified in the little houses listening to stories of the White Lady who was reported to have haunted the mill and neighbourhood. There were also tales of a headless horseman who galloped around the area in the early morning. The older members of the community testified that they often encountered Galloper Thompson, as the strange horseman was known in the local folklore, as they went through the dark streets at about 5.30 in the morning.

The stories of the White Lady were conflicting. Some took her appearances as an omen of impending danger. 'Something is going to happen' was a common remark when someone reported seeing her. At the other end of the scale, stories were told of miraculous escapes when unseen hands prevented young girls from being caught up in whirling machinery. I often wondered if she gave any warning that night of the impending danger.

We had lost trace of time but we must have been working from place to place for about three hours. The work was fatiguing as we climbed through debris or trudged through smoke-filled streets littered with debris and sewage. The scenes we met with were horrific. There was death and destruction everywhere. Our equipment seemed to get heavier and more awkward to carry. Streets that we had passed through previously were now littered with debris and houses were burning here and there. I wondered despairingly if it was ever going to finish. It was now around 3 or 4 o'clock. In fact we were to endure another three hours of this hell. We selected a few fires which we felt we could contain. Quick action was necessary when these small houses caught fire. They burned like tinder. There was little we could do. Our stirrup pumps and buckets could not prevent the rapid spread of fire. In these circumstances it was necessary to ensure that no one was trapped, or that some distracted householder did not make an attempt to enter the burning house to recover some treasured article. In some cases they just wanted to return to their home whatever the risk.

Finally we came back to the post and made our reports. It was good to get a rest and escape, if only for a few minutes, from the carnage and misery we had just left. The end, however, was far off. We had only faced half of our ordeal. I took this opportunity to go to the shelter to see my family. I was bombarded with questions from the others as to what it was like outside. I told them it was bad, without going into details, but I knew that some of them had lost relatives and friends. One, I knew for sure, had lost a brother and his family. I thought it better to keep this information from them. They would have many problems to face when they came out of the shelter. I, too, would have my own personal problems but I could not let them worry me at that moment.

I took part in many rescue operations that night and during the following days. One of the simplest rescues in which I was engaged still amuses me because I have heard the story told so often and in so many ways. The family concerned always thought of me as their hero. There was nothing heroic or spectacular in the affair. The blast from exploding bombs blew doors off their hinges even at a distance and when I was passing these houses I went in and shouted 'Is anyone here?' In one of these houses, in reply to my call, a voice came back, 'Yes, we are over here. We are buried.' I ran over to the door of the cupboard which led to the little space under the stairs. The door was jammed by pieces of plaster which had fallen from the ceiling. I kicked the plaster away with my foot and opened the door. It was so simple that I thought nothing of it. The family, however, saw it in a different light. They had tried to get out and were convinced that they were trapped for good: a terrifying experience. There were six of them in a confined space and if they had not been discovered until the next day or had they panicked who knows what may have happened.

We carried out many simple operations which must have helped many unfortunate families who were so gripped with fear that it affected their normal reasoning. As I came in contact with manifest panic and fear, I was glad and thankful that I had become involved with A.R.P. Our duties gave us a sense of responsibility and prevented us from dwelling on the dangers to which we were exposed ourselves. There were a few narrow escapes during the night and in the closing hours of the raid we just hoped that our luck would hold out.

We had been in the open all night while bombs fell only a few yards or minutes from us as we moved about. How we escaped I do not know.

5 The closing hours

Our impromptu flying squad was on the move again. We were at the corner of Cranburn Street waiting for some wardens who had gone to the post with reports and to collect a few more buckets and stirrup pumps. Fires had started in the Fleetwood Street area. The houses there were of a more substantial nature than those of the little mill type houses we had been working at and gave a better chance of success in saving some of them. While we were standing at the corner, we heard the whistle of bombs as they came down in our direction. My experience during the night made me alert to danger. I shouted 'Take cover! The shelter!' There was a shelter on the other corner but we knew we could not make the entrance or if we did we would block it in a wild attempt to get through. With only seconds to spare we threw ourselves to the ground behind the far side of the shelter.

It was lucky for us that we picked this position because any other one would have resulted in our being blown to pieces. We lay there huddled together waiting with bated breath for the expected upheaval. Three bombs came crashing down close together. They were heavy ones and caused extensive damage. A complete block of shops opposite to where we were standing was left in ruins. On our left, at the other end of the shelter, a large garage, showrooms and offices were demolished and the ruins were in flames. A little to our right, Pim Street was partially destroyed. As we lay behind the shelter there was a dreadful silence. Only those who have waited for an impending explosion or some other threat of death can really understand. For us time had stopped. Then came the roar of the explosion and the ground beneath us shook and vibrated. We could hear the awful screech and grinding as timber and brickwork were torn apart, and finally the scattered sounds of falling masonry and tinkling glass as the force of the explosion spent itself. Then again there came a deep silence. It was a silence so uncanny, so complete, we could scarcely believe we were alive. I felt responsible for my companions. They had followed me and worked under my directions without the least thought for their own safety. For the second time that night I had saved my own life and those with me had survived too. Three bombs came down just a few yards from us and I had managed to direct six men from what would have been certain death to safety.

We stood up a little shaken but alert and went into the shelter to see if everything was all right. No one was hurt but they were extremely frightened. They had heard the explosions and could feel the shelter shake. Later in the night we heard of several disasters when shelters collapsed. There were about fifty people including many children in that shelter and in spite of the lack of amenities it had protected my family and neighbours twice during the night. The early type of shelter had no supporting walls inside. If one received a direct blast, the walls collapsed and the roof, which was a solid mass of reinforced concrete, came crashing down and crushed everyone inside. In incidents involving shelters many perished during the night.

So much had happened in a few seconds, it was unbelievable, but now the wardens were back with their stirrup pumps and buckets. They came running down the street and were overjoyed and surprised to see us all alive. At least they expected to find us injured or slashed by flying glass from the car showrooms or the large shop windows on the other side of the street. Now there was more damage to contend with. A few other wardens came down from the post to see what had happened to us. I directed them to investigate the damage at Pim Street and to report back to the post that we were all safe and on our way to Fleetwood Street. Here we met with a strong concentration of coal and sewer gas due to burst mains. Houses were burning in the small network of streets comprising the area and, as we expected, we were successful in this stronger type of building, as the fires did not spread so quickly. Some, however, got out of control and we had to

abandon our efforts. The heavy concentration of gas fumes in
the Carlisle Circus area caused some concern and two workmen collapsed and died. One was found dead by one of his
workmates in a temporary latrine put up for the workmen.
Someone directed us to a house where we discovered an
elderly lady who was overcome by gas fumes and in need of
medical attention. The Mater Hospital was close by and
instead of wasting time looking for an ambulance we decided
to bring her there ourselves.

It was our first visit to the hospital and we were shocked at
what we saw. The Mater was a voluntary hospital with only a
small staff of nurses and doctors. It was never expected that it
would be called upon to face such a task as it did. Every
available bed was occupied and makeshift beds were squeezed
into the wards, but still the steady flow of ambulances brought
more and more injured. The overflow of casualties spread out
into the corridors. Every piece of space was pressed into use.
Even the stretchers on which casualties were carried served as
emergency beds. The scenes could best be described as being
similar to the field hospitals set up by Florence Nightingale
during the Crimean War. The injured still wore their grimy
and bloodstained clothing. Some were lying quietly but, overall, the wards and corridors were filled with moans and
screams of the injured. I asked myself how could anyone sort
out this mass of human suffering? One alarming feature was
the distressed relatives who were milling around in search of
information about their friends. Staff, overworked doctors and
nurses moved about trying to diagnose and relieve pain where
they possibly could.

As we looked about us, we could only see a gigantic jig-saw
puzzle. It is a fact, however, that every group, some way or
another, finds a method for doing the impossible, otherwise
nothing would ever be accomplished. Here the doctors and
nurses were going about the task of doing the impossible as
best they could. Outside, the other services were doing their
jobs and the overworked hospitals were kept busy as the
ambulance men continued to bring in more and more casualties. These were the men who faced the full dangers of the
night as they dashed through the dark, debris littered and
sometimes blazing streets and on occasions narrowly missed

bombs as they went to collect the injured whom firemen, rescue services and wardens handed over to their care. Unfortunately, some of the civil defence workers did not escape the bombs and some ambulance men were among those who died.

The hospitals in the city handled over 2,000 casualties of whom about 600 were classified as serious. It is worth noting that the number of dead, somewhere in the region of 900, was more than the number of seriously injured.

Our business at the hospital was finished and, like our medical comrades, we too had a gigantic jig-saw puzzle to put together. As we came out, the hospital itself was under attack. Incendiary bombs were burning on the roof and pathways. While doctors and nurses worked feverishly to save lives inside, firemen were working desperately to fight the flames that were licking so dangerously around it.

Our flying squad had scored some successes but compared to the death and destruction all around us, together with the number of injured we had just seen, our efforts had only scratched the surface. Our greatest achievement, we felt, was that by our very presence we were able to help and calm the fears of the frightened community. The wardens gave their best but numbers were far too few to meet the onslaught. We just had to continue our battle alone, eight young men sustained by the thought that surely the night must come to an end and that help, so urgently needed to remove the mountains of debris, would soon arrive.

We were tired now as we climbed over the debris hoping to hear a sound, but the bombs had been too strong and the little houses too weak to offer any resistance. With the exception of minor injuries and cases of hysteria we met death everywhere we went. The events of the night were beginning to take their toll on our minds and bodies. Dawn was breaking and in the morning light the sound of the planes still above us was less frightening even though the clearer view of the damage was more alarming. Even during our short stay at the Mater Hospital new fires had started in the Carlisle Circus area. The whole situation began to appear like the re-run of a frightening film and the feeling of abandonment that haunted us added to the horror of the events. Tired and lonely we moved again through the area, making contact with the wardens on patrol who like ourselves felt isolated. In vain we watched and listened for the assistance we had so urgently requested.

From time to time we picked up scraps of news: fact or rumour, it did not matter. It was the only source of communication available to us. Into this melting pot of fact and fiction came the news that a contingent of firemen from Dublin, Dundalk and Drogheda had crossed the border in spite of Southern Ireland's neutrality and were now active in the city, and more help was on its way from Glasgow and Liverpool. The city centre was badly smashed, fires were raging and bombs continued to fall even as the firemen fought the flames. This additional help greatly enhanced the spirits of the local firemen who were fighting to the point of exhaustion to control or contain the fires that threatened to engulf the entire city centre.

By 6 o'clock we felt that the raid could not last much longer and we started to think up plans for the coming day. We did not have any ropes and we knew they would be needed to cordon off some dangerous over-hanging buildings before people started moving around. Montague and I said that we would go down to Victoria Barracks and try to get some from the army. Although we were civilians the guards permitted us to enter. We saw damage and carnage and heard reports that no civilian or press representatives were allowed to see or report on.

The barrack complex was devastated. Large blocks were in ruins, some of them blazing. The married quarters received a direct hit resulting in heavy casualties and loss of life. Rescue teams were busily engaged trying to recover bodies or others who could be brought out alive. This was the sight that met us as we passed along with one of the guards from the gate who directed us through the area and gave us a running commentary as we went along. We could see more new fires were blazing fiercely in the buildings used as stores. 'The gunners collected a packet' was how our guide described a direct hit on a gun crew. A group of A.T.S. girls perished in this attack as did some more when a bomb hit their quarters. Our informant told us that about 30 A.T.S. were killed. He told us of further major damage at the far end of the barrack, as we cut off between two large blocks. I have already described the early attack on the barracks when I was caught nearby with a companion and what we saw now of the extent of the damage confirmed our fears. In the face of all this devastation our own troubles seemed to diminish and we felt ashamed to ask for the ropes. However they had plenty and gave us some without any bother.

'Did you have anything to eat during the night?' someone asked. I almost laughed as I thought how we had spent the night. 'Not much time to think of eating,' I said. 'I suppose you're right, mate,' he replied. 'But it must be surely near an end. Those Jerries sure had a picnic up there all night. Let's go over to the cookhouse, they will be brewing something up over there.' The cookhouse was the most relaxed place we had been all night. From the atmosphere it would have been hard to guess that we were in the middle of a full scale blitz. The soldiers spoke with a pleasant accent that even made their swear words sound different to our ears. One of the boys brought us a large mug of cocoa and a cheese sandwich. I shall never forget that simple meal. A big fellow just cut into a loaf and sliced a piece of cheese as thick as the bread itself and clamped it between the two slices. As for the cocoa, the soldier who brought it over laughed and said 'That's real army stuff, mate.' It was certainly thick and the sugar must have been put in with a shovel. It was the first time that night that I felt hungry and Montague and I ate heartily. It was like a banquet and I am sure if we had been served with a full meal we would not have had the appetite for it.

We chatted for a while. I think they enjoyed our company and our accents. 'Don't they speak funny,' one of them said and we all laughed. The flow of conversation helped to break the tension and although death was all around us it seemed as if we were in a different world. It transpired that the big fellow who made the sandwiches was not the regular cook nor were we in the cookhouse. The cook and his staff were dead. 'They collected one during the night' was the expression used to explain their deaths. Apparently the cookhouse took a direct hit and all inside were killed.

Breakfast, according to the big fellow, would be no prize winning menu. 'The so and so's will get what I can gather up.'

He seemed to enjoy his thoughts on the menu he was putting together. The conversation was good with a mixture of serious talk and witty remarks. It was almost daylight outside and we said we would have to go and get on with the job of roping off the dangerous buildings we had noted. We picked up our ropes, wished our friends good luck, and went out into the early morning light. All around us there was some activity as soldiers moved about their duties. Heavy billows of smoke and flames were still coming from buildings as the fires got out of control. It gave us a strange feeling to witness this as civilians. As the name would suggest, Victoria Barracks was an old military establishment and had been in the area for about a hundred years and very few civilians had ever been inside it. But here we were at a moment of top security and censorship getting a conducted tour of the damage. The soldier who walked us back to the gate pointed out and explained the major sites of damage. He swung his arms in a circle pointing out places where his mates were killed.

We were two lonely figures as we made our way through the debris at Carlisle Circus with the heavy coils of rope slung over our shoulders. As we walked along talking and joking about the cocoa and the sandwiches and the attitude of the soldiers back at the barracks, suddenly it struck us that for the past half hour we had been in one of the most dangerous places in Belfast. The conversation had been so easy going and the atmosphere so relaxed that we had not given a thought to what we had always regarded as a potentially dangerous area. We guessed that the soldiers had seen death on a large scale before, but for us it was something new and something we would have to learn to live with.

It was already clear daylight, but a heavy haze of smoke hanging over the city cut out the rays of the early morning sun. We had started roping off dangerous areas when the all clear was sounded. Church bells ringing in the New Year never sounded so joyful.

Trinity Street Church, 12 July, 1941.   (Ulster Museum Garland Collection)
This scene of devastation was caused when a parachute mine caught the spire of the church on the night of Easter Tuesday, 1941. The heavy granite masonry crashed down on the Trinity Street wardens' post killing everyone inside. (See pages 26–9)

6　The mortuary

The raid was over, but for the civil defence a mammoth task involving every aspect of human misery was yet to be faced and a few of our wardens, including myself, came face to face with a situation grimmer and more horrible than anything we had experienced during the raid.

For the moment the job in hand was to get an up-to-date appraisal of the post area. The night had been a terrifying experience for us all and now, thank God, we were all back at the post. We were tired, cut, blistered and bruised, our clothes stained with sewage and blood. Everyone was at once scared, excited and relieved. It was a great sight to see all our friends and one that will live for ever in my memory.

Our plan of action was again a simple one. We went out on a quick reconnaissance and took care of some more casualties. We spoke to as many people as possible and told them to come to the post later, by which time we would have information about welfare arrangements. We advised them to reject rumours and to keep away from any suspicious articles, even something in their own homes which may have come through the window or roof. We tried to share the feeling that as members of the same community we had suffered just as they. This was one of the feelings that had haunted us all night; these were our neighbours, we must help them as best we could.

Rescue teams arrived and went to work on sites where people were known to be trapped. The fires had burned out and now only the bare skeletons remained of what had been the homes and small shops of the neighbourhood. It was a depressing scene. The district had never been graced with any buildings of historical interest but the whole area held a niche

in history. It sprang up during the Industrial Revolution and
bore all the structural marks of its time, the narrow, cobbled
streets and rows of back-to-back one up and one down houses.
As we looked over the district that we knew so well and that
held many childhood memories for us, it seemed to be
doomed. At that moment we could not possibly have realised
the strength and resolve of the people after they had got over
their initial shock.

Everywhere we experienced the tears, the sorrow and the
near hysteria of relatives, as they stood gazing at the heaps of
rubble that encased their loved ones. I could well understand
how they felt. Just a few hours ago I had stood broken-hearted
beside a similar pile of rubble, thinking my parents and sister
were beneath it.

I detailed some wardens to patrol the areas of damage and to
act as guides for any services arriving at the sites. The others
returned to the post to prepare for the flood of homeless
victims whom we knew would soon be on our doorstep. D
District had taken an unbelievable hammering. The death toll
was high. At least half of these casualties came from our own
post area and the streets on our immediate boundaries.

Messages and information regarding emergency arrangements, rest centres, telephone numbers and related matters
arrived at the post and McQuillan, our post artist, prepared a
set of large cards displaying the telephone numbers and
addresses of the emergency welfare offices. While we were
preparing to set up an inquiry and information post, we
received an urgent appeal for volunteers to go to the Falls Road
Baths which were being used as an emergency mortuary. The
message stressed that the work would be strenuous and
unpleasant and that only those who felt they could undertake
such work should volunteer. Three of us volunteered to go,
John Montague, Cyril Kelly and myself. There was no public
transport so we set off on foot.

The walk brought us through another part of the city that
had come under attack during the night. We passed by the old
church in Eglinton Street. It was used as an army billet and
received a direct hit which killed about 30 soldiers and some
civilians in nearby houses. This incident created a great deal of
curiosity and attracted a lot more activity than other sites of

damage. During the night a rumour spread that a plane had been shot down and crashed in Eglinton Street. There were no telephones but this was one message that spread throughout the city. The actual facts were as follows. As I said, the old church was an army billet and in the forecourt there were a number of heavy army transport trucks. An initial inspection of the incident in the darkness revealed the great wheels and parts of the heavy chassis of the trucks which people thought were parts of a plane. This was the foundation of the rumour which still circulates and I have even seen it referred to in newspaper articles.

We went on and passed through a mass of little streets known as the Hammer. It was here that we met up with firemen from the South of Ireland. They were fighting a fire at a large government food storage depot in Hudson Street. Rivers of margarine, butter and lard were flowing down the streets. It was an hilarious scene as the firemen and ourselves slipped and slid in the sticky mess as we moved along.

It was one of the remarkable occurrences of the blitz, that several brigades from the fire service in the south should have responded to the call for help and driven many miles to risk their lives fighting fires in Belfast.

We left the Irish firemen on the Shankill Road and went down Percy Street, the scene of the greatest disaster of the raid. A shelter had suffered a direct hit and about 70 people were killed when it collapsed. I knew many of those who died. When I was serving my apprenticeship in that area, I had walked up Percy Street every evening. One of the women standing close by remembered me and recalled my friendship with a young girl who lived in the street. She was very pretty and she often waited for me as I came out of the workshop. The older boys chaffed me about this but, as I have said, she was very pretty and I was proud that she had singled me out from the other boys. She was in the shelter when the bomb hit it. I swallowed hard and held back a tear. My memory went back to those days and my first day at work. But we had to push on, so I wished the old woman goodbye and we continued down the debris strewn street towards the Falls Road.

We were getting nearer to the baths and the long, grim, heartbreaking experiences that never will be forgotten. It was about 8 a.m. when we arrived. We expected a similar scene to that at the Mater Hospital where relatives were milling around searching for news of families or friends. This morning, however, there were no crowds and comparatively few people. On our way in, the first shock of the morning was the sight of a burned hand lying in the doorway, but there was more to come. We had volunteered but we were totally unprepared for the real horror that was to follow. Hundreds of bodies brought in from scattered incidents were lying all around us. They were men and women, young people, children and infants. How could anyone have visualised seeing so many broken bodies in one place? No text books, no training pamphlets could have prepared us for the grim task we were about to undertake. Some were whole and others hardly resembled human beings. The scene could only be compared in a small way to the pictures released some years later of the mass graves at Belsen and other German death camps.

Any information that could help to identify the unfortunate victims was recorded. Watches, rings, photographs and other personal effects were listed to help with identification. Details of where bodies were found were not always useful in establishing identity. In many cases they were killed on their way home and they were found in areas far from their own districts and among strangers. Bodies were laid out in plain, box-like coffins. Mothers and infants were laid out together just as they had been found. We could imagine a mother clutching her baby close to her as the bombs fell. The baths were intended to be used as a mortuary where people could go to identify the dead but it became too crowded. The baths were drained and the bodies were put down on to the tiled floor of the pool but still more and more came in.

The air was filled with the stench of dead bodies and a heavy concentration of disinfectant. Some of the workers took sick. Our experience of handling dead and mutilated bodies during the raid in some way prepared us and we were able to carry on. Montague and Kelly were great fellows. We had been together all night and I think we lent strength to each other; again it came to me forcibly that one can work better under stress with reliable friends. We did not speak much as we went about our work. We were alone with our thoughts. I speculated on what was happening at the post and, above all, what was going to happen to-night? This was the thought that everyone in Belfast must have had in mind, what would happen as darkness came?

Meanwhile, more bodies arrived and the work became more and more ghastly. These later bodies were mutilated and beginning to decompose due to the nature of their injuries. The task of sorting them out became too much for some of the volunteers and they had to leave but those who remained seemed to get new strength and we doubled our efforts. The work was heavy. Our backs and arm muscles ached as we lifted and carried the lifeless bodies.

I was thirsty, the smell of burned and decomposed flesh was in my nostrils and there was a horrible taste in my mouth. Even to this day the smell and taste returns to me occasionally. We did not stop for lunch but someone kept an urn of tea stewing in a room near the entrance. It was horrible stuff but at least it helped to moisten my tongue which at times because as dry and tough as leather.

Somehow I always remember one of the corpses. It was that of a very hefty policeman. He had been caught in the blast of an explosion. His injuries were internal. His outer appearance showed no signs of injury but we could see as we lifted him that he was bleeding internally. We saw every type of injury but they all resulted in death. To me the tales of Edgar Allen Poe fell short when compared with this real house of horror.

We were in the baths for six hours or more and the work was gradually coming to an end. It was intended to use the baths as the only mortuary but it proved to be too small. Other arrangements had to be made, and the bodies were removed to St George's Market and were set out there for the public to come and identify them. They remained there for several days and distracted relatives gazed on countless victims in the hope that they could recognise their friends and loved ones. Every assistance was given to help in the identification. Articles such as watches, rings and photographs found on the victims were shown to inquirers. In many cases the bodies were beyond recognition. In other cases the victims had lost touch with their families and relations and there was no one to mourn or recognise them.

At last the operation had to be brought to a close, and on the 22nd April the remaining victims were buried. There were 150 unidentified victims. Those who had Rosary beads or other Catholic religious articles were buried in Milltown Cemetery, the others were laid to rest in the City Cemetery. A service was conducted by church dignitaries from the different denominations including the Jewish community. In attendance was the Governor, The Duke of Abercorn, members of the government, the Lord Mayor and members of the council, as well as thousands of ordinary citizens who lined the streets. People wept and stood to attention as the solemn procession passed through the city.

This was the sequence of events which followed the gruesome work at the baths. It had been fatiguing and a nightmare, but it was something that had to be done and as we made our way back to the post we could not help but feel that we had performed a worthwhile task.

7   The homeless

Our work at the mortuary was finished and as we made our way back through the narrow streets we could see that the scene had changed dramatically from that of the early morning. People were no longer standing or wandering about aimlessly. The little groups of inquisitive bystanders had given way to masses of people all on the move. There were complete families, old people, young couples and children. Their every action reflected the fear and panic that was growing among them. They moved along hurriedly, grasping parcels, suitcases, baskets and anything capable of holding their most treasured possessions. Others were pushing prams loaded with bed-clothes and other essentials. We had seen the effects of panic during the night. It was a terrible thing, robbing people of all sense of reason, and here we were witnessing it again. It set us thinking. If this was the reaction in this part of the city, which had been only slightly scratched in the raid, what would be the situation in our own district which had been battered from end to end? The very thought was frightening. It seemed as if the whole city was on the move.

At Carlisle Circus we caught up with a moving mass of people whose only motivation was fear. There was no transport yet in the city. The crowds were making their way on foot, struggling with anything they could carry that would be of use. Frightened and bewildered children held on tightly to their favourite toys as anxious mothers pulled them along by the hand. They were all heading for the railway and bus stations. The more determined were pulling handcarts, piled high with furniture, and in some cases children were sitting perched on chairs which were securely tied in position. The scenes were reminiscent of the early days of the war when the

roads throughout western Europe were thronged with
refugees fleeing from the advancing German Panzer divisions.
The determination of those pulling the handcarts was amazing. I knew one fellow who pulled a fully loaded handcart to
the far side of Ballymena, a distance of about 40 miles.

When we arrived back to the post there was pandemonium.
The place was crowded with frightened and confused residents of the area. Some of them only required information but,
unfortunately, most of them wanted miracles. We knew their
fear was real and their needs were genuine. They were under
great strain and had come through a terrible experience. They
needed our help and reassurance.

While we read up on the welfare arrangements someone
brought us a cup of tea and a piece of bread. With the exception
of the stewed tea at the mortuary this was the first food I had
since the cocoa and sandwich I got in the barracks. We studied
the various forms and the particulars we were required to get
from applicants.

There were vouchers for rest centres, travel vouchers, petrol
ration coupons and certificates which classified a person as
homeless. This was a new type of work for the most of us, but
the welfare service was snowed under and some of the work
was handed over to the wardens as it was thought we already
had a good relationship with our local communities.

The wardens had the authority to issue a certificate of
homelessness to genuine victims of the blitz. The welfare and
benefits machinery set up to deal with emergency claims
depended in the early stages on the proper control of these
certificates. They were, in fact, a certified introduction to the
various government offices set up to administer initial welfare
grants. It did not take long for the confidence tricksters to
realise the potential value of certificates and this was a new
problem we had to face, but we were determined to beat them
and we kept a strict check on these rogues and their schemes.
This situation did not develop until a few days later and I will
describe later on how we organised ourselves to combat these
leeches.

Our present problem was to listen to the people who now
thronged the offices. We could give no material or financial
help. We could only interview the applicants and help them to

fill in the appropriate forms or write them out for them, which in most cases we did. We endorsed these forms with the post stamp and directed the applicants to the welfare officer. The plan was straightforward but like all plans it met with difficulties. The welfare service was faced with an enormous burden, which to their credit they handled magnificently. In all, volunteers, including the Women's Voluntary Service, supplied 70,000 meals and organised shelter at rest centres for 40,000 homeless. They helped to trace and prepare documentation for 100,000 people who, according to estimates, left Belfast either through welfare offices or by their own arrangements.

At times it seemed hopeless to explain that we could not supply transport or local accommodation. We pointed out to people that their best plan was to go to the welfare office with our form and that all possible help would be given to them and emergency accommodation for that night at least. As I have already said, they were looking for miracles which we were unable to perform. In these circumstances it was difficult to be firm and at the same time to take care to avoid offending or annoying anyone. It was exhausting to sit there for hours going over the same ground and, as we looked around, the crowd did not seem to diminish. Sometimes we were able to get our information across without any difficulty but in most cases we had to explain many times over. I can recall arguments that broke out among the people when it was thought that someone was taking up too much time at the table. It struck us as funny that while we were trying to be patient, it was they themselves that were irritable. Looking back, however, it was quite understandable, as they too were under severe stress.

It was approaching evening by the time we finished. 'I'd rather go through the blitz than meet that crowd again,' said one of the wardens when we had settled down. We were enjoying the rest and the conversation was good, when a report came in that some shops on the Antrim Road had re-ignited. I said I would go down and see. I thought that a little action would help to relieve the tension of the day's work. Two other lads joined me, and armed with axes and pumps we went out on a small firefighting exercise.

We were in one of the shops damping down some smolder-

ing timbers when I heard a voice calling 'Is Jim Doherty there?'
It was my girlfriend, my future wife. She was living in Bally-
clare at the time and she and her friend had come up to see me.
I came out of the shop and I must have looked a sorry sight. I
had worked all night and all that day. I did not have a change
of clothing. The clothes I wore were wet and covered with mud
and bloodstains. I needed to shave and my eyes were red and
burning with the smoke in the old shop.

She was glad to see me and in spite of my appearance she
flung her arms around me in a fond embrace. I lifted her and
swung her around with a feeling of sheer delight. She said she
went to see me and saw the house in ruins. Fearing the worst
she went off in search of information about me and my family.
It was a great re-union. I told her the family was safe and that
they were with friends in the country. Father was with me and
we were stopping at the post until we could get somewhere
permanent to live.

I thought it would be difficult for them to get home but just
how difficult I had not imagined. 'Wait a few minutes until I
finish this job,' I said, 'and I will go with you to the station.'
Smithfield bus station was an amazing scene. Hundreds of
people were milling around with only one thought in mind.
They wanted to be away from the city before nightfall. 'Nightfall' was the magic word. It was the driving force that gave
them the energy to walk for miles and the strength to carry
suitcases that at normal times they would not even have
attempted to lift. Station staff struggled with enquiries which
came at them from all directions. In many cases people had
only the name of some remote place and had no idea of its
location. The traffic clerks and inspectors were not prepared
for this kind of situation and in many cases had never even
heard of some of the places people wanted to go. Greater still
was the confusion when people were told they were at the
wrong station.

The major problem, of course, was that there was just not
sufficient transport to cope with the emergency. Any kind of
transport was pressed into use. I saw cattle lorries being
washed, disinfected and fresh straw strewn on the floors.
Those who did not intend to travel too far eagerly sought
places in these and soon they were also filled. The crowd grew

uneasy and in sheer panic began to lose their sense of discipline. As buses moved on to the departure platforms the crowd surged forward. I could see that, as it got later, things could get out of hand and I advised the girls to take any bus that would leave them within a reasonable walking distance from home. Almost an hour passed before they were able to find something going their way. To witness the scenes at the bus station was an experience, to be forced to be part of it was an entirely different story.

Air Raid Precautions

Belfast Civil Defence Authority

District ..D........
Post No. .38.1....
Date ..17.. 4.. 41

This is to certify that: .MRS...W.H.I.T.E.......
of .....2.6..GREEN...STREET.....BELFAST

Was rendered ~~Temporarily~~ / Completely Homeless*

As a result of Enemy Action.

Post Warden's Signature W.B.lack

Post Stamp

Delete where inapplicable*

A specimen of a certificate issued by the wardens to a homeless person.

(Doherty Collection)

8   Welfare work and rest centres

Back at the post the hubbub and excitement had settled down.
The crowds were gone and the streets were silent; with the
exception of a few families scattered over the area the neighbourhood was deserted. The wardens were sitting resting and
some were sleeping on the floor. I lay down on the floor myself
and shook off my boots. It was a great feeling to be relaxed.
Someone brought me a cup of tea and a slice of bread. There
was no scarcity of tea but supplies of bread and milk were a
problem that was to exist in the city for the rest of the week.

The group warden, like ourselves, had not rested for the
past two days. Unlike many other group wardens, Brian
Gillespie did not believe in useless discipline. Certain rules
had to be observed, but he felt that the important discipline
came from within ourselves. Post 381 had a spirit all of its own
which in some way made it different. We did not have the
badge wearing mentality which, unfortunately, many other
A.R.P. volunteers had. District officers and top brass seldom
came near us although they always used our volunteers for
important demonstrations or exercises. In fact, as I will explain
later, Post 381 in open competition won the trophy and title for
being the most outstanding post in Northern Ireland.

Now our group warden was preparing patrols and, of
course, there was still the fear that German bombers would be
over again that night and we had to make plans. It was our
intention to keep the patrols going throughout the area during
the night. This was for the benefit of those who were still in the
area. It was going to be a long night. The wardens were already
exhausted, but rotas were drawn up and the first patrols went
out. My old mate Howey was appointed post warden and I
teamed up again with Montague. It was about nine o'clock and

as we passed Carlisle Circus we noticed that a sizeable crowd was assembling. They did not live in the area and were complete strangers to us and to each other. They were people who had decided earlier to stay in their own homes but, for some reason, at this late hour had changed their minds. Whether it was rumours, or a sudden feeling of fear or loneliness did not really matter to us. The fact was that they were in our area and we felt it was our duty to assist them. It was an unforeseen problem for which we could offer no immediate solution. Montague went back to the post to report this new development. I felt I could handle the crowd and remained behind to talk to them and tried to find out where they came from.

There were no cars on the road. Anyone who owned a car had left earlier but at any rate I had decided that it would not be safe to stop cars to get lifts for one or two people. My experience at the bus station suggested that in all probability the crowd would all rush at the first car that stopped. The only answer was a lorry or a truck so I had decided that I would go and see what the army could do for us. Montague returned with two other wardens. I explained that I was going to the barracks to try to get some transport and warned them not to stop any cars which might come by. After telling the crowd that we were going to enquire about any available transport and assuring them that we would be back, Montague and I set off.

The barracks was under strict security, but one of the guards recognised us. 'Hello, Paddy' he greeted us and introduced us to his friends. 'These are the two mad Irish blokes I was telling you about.' Our visit during the raid must have impressed the soldiers or at least it had given them a topic for conversation. We told them that we had a panicky crowd who had assembled at Carlisle Circus and that we needed some transport to bring them out to Glengormley. A rest centre was established in the Barron Hall and if we could get them out to it, they would be all right until morning.

'That's something the big fellow himself would have to handle,' said one of the guards. 'Come, I'll bring you to him. He's a right bloke; at least he'll listen to you.' The clearing up squads had done a great job. The fires which were blazing had all burned out, some buildings had already been demolished and the debris was cleared away. The place did not appear so devastated as it did when we saw it last. Our guide brought us to the quarters of the Provost Marshal, who at the time was Major Green. He listened to our story but said he was sorry, all his transport was away. I pressed him further and asked if he would possibly have any later on. He did not reply, instead he went to his cupboard and took out a red sash and cap. He was already in uniform and the sash lent a dash of colour and authority to his appearance. 'Show me where these people are and I will go and speak with them,' he said. 'Are there any cars on the road?'

I could see now that putting on his sash was part of a plan to persuade any motorised transport to stop, or should I say intimidate them to stop. It was growing dark and the crowd was becoming increasingly restless. The road was deserted, not a car had passed nor were there likely to be any. The Major was beginning to show some concern. 'We do have a problem here,' he said. It was a problem that had no solution other than a five mile walk along a dark, lonely road. The crowd was made up of women and young children and men of different age groups. Most of them were carrying some kind of parcels. Chance, that strange factor that appears from time to time in impossible situations, came to our assistance. As we were talking with the Major we could hear the heavy labouring sound of a large vehicle coming up Clifton Street. The Major was excited. 'This is it,' he said and stepped out and waved it down. The truck screeched to a stop. It was an army transport and a young soldier jumped down from the cabin and stood stiffly to attention. The Major put him at his ease and asked where he was going. He was on his way to Ballymena. His duty was finished and he was returning to base. 'What have you in the truck?' asked the Major. 'Nothing, Sir,' he replied sharply, still somewhat nervous in the presence of the Major. 'Good! Good! Very good, just what we want,' said the Major. He explained to the driver that he wanted him to take the people standing there to wherever we wished him to go. He took his papers and wrote something on them, at the same time telling him we had his authority to sign the papers when we dismissed him.

We piled the crowd into the truck. It was not comfortable but it was transport and they were thankful that they would not have to spend the night in the city. The Major shook hands with us. He was extremely pleased with his part in the affair and went away laughing and waving to us. The soldier was still a little nervous after his encounter with the Major and continued to address us as sir. 'Who was that?' he enquired. 'Major Green, Provost Marshal,' I replied in a rather stiff mocking tone of voice that made him smile and put him at ease.

'The lads will never believe it when I tell them. That was the Provost Marshal, you said?'

I laughed and replied 'Indeed that was the man himself.'

I climbed into the back with the people and John went up front with the driver to give him directions. The rest of the wardens returned to the post and reported that we were away to the rest centre at Glengormley and told the story about the crowd of people and the Major. That journey was the most uncomfortable one I have ever experienced. We were thrown about every time the truck hit a pot-hole or crossed a sunken tram track. As we continued on our way I was convinced that the truck had square wheels. It was the only logical explanataion that could account for the way we were being thrown about as we were. The passengers were wonderful once they had put their fears behind them, especially the women. They sang all the way, at the top of their voices. I can well remember one of the songs which they sang over and over again. It was an old mill ditty that they had adapted for the occasion and it went as follows:

> Hitler thought he had us with his Ya, Ya, Ya.
> Hitler thought he had us with his Ya, Ya, Ya.
> Hitler thought he had us
> But you see he never got us
> With his Ya, Ya, Ya.

Finally we arrived at the Barron Hall. The centre was packed out but the welfare ladies made us welcome and soon we were served with hot tea and sandwiches. We enjoyed the meal. Like ourselves, the soldier had been working all day without a proper meal. When he finished he said he would have to go. I signed his papers and entered the time he left as directed by the Major. We wished him good-night and off he went to Ballymena.

We stayed a little while with the folk until they had registered and we reported why we brought them to the centre, and then we had to go. It was about midnight and the place was deserted. There was no hope of any transport going towards Belfast, so we decided to walk. As we trudged along in the darkness we were tired and we tripped and stumbled on the uneven road. The Antrim Road leading out to Glengormley at that time was little better than a country lane and was in no way comparable to our beautiful wide road today.

I was completely exhausted. I had been on my feet for two hectic days. I had faced death twice. There had been the work on the bomb sites where we had taken out the dead and the living as well as our ordeal at the mortuary. My feet were sore. I did not even have a change of socks. Everything I owned was buried under the pile of rubble that was once my home. Any money I had was buried along with my possessions. I had not a penny in my pocket, but all that seemed to matter was rest. I just wanted to sleep. We made it back to the post about 2 o'clock in the morning. My feet felt as if they were cut to pieces. I asked someone to pull off my boots and I lay down on the floor and fell fast alseep. I woke early, feeling refreshed. Others had joined me during the night on the floor and some were sleeping on the benches. It was a comforting sight. I was proud to be a part of this group of great fellows.

There was no gas and we made a fire with sticks, and brewed a pot of tea. Someone produced a piece of bread. It was stale, but we spread it liberally with jam. There was no milk to be bought and what we had was sour, so we took the tea black. It was a rough breakfast but it suited the circumstances. There were at least a dozen of us living at the post. Our families had gone away or our houses were destroyed or badly damaged.

I knew I would have to get some clean clothes and a bath and a shave. I could not go through another day in my present state. We went out on an early patrol. It was about 7 o'clock and as we moved through the streets the locals greeted us. Other wardens had kept contact with them during the night and like ourselves they did not go to bed but just dozed off sitting in their chairs. It was good to see them looking so settled and not frightened. The first night in the ghost town had passed quietly. On our return to the post I decided to go down to the old house and make a determined effort to rescue some of my clothes before the day really started.

I was joined by about six or seven of the gang and we moved off like a squad of navvies carrying ropes, picks and shovels. The upper storeys and staircase had collapsed but I located what I thought was my bedroom in the heart of a mountain of rubble. The whole row of houses had collapsed like a pack of cards when a parachute mine exploded at the rear in Lincoln Avenue. We started to clear the debris and the gang worked as if a life depended on their efforts. The idea of digging for my clothes and other belongings was great fun for them and excitement grew as we unearthed the wardrobe and a chest of drawers. As they saw it, they thought of it as digging for buried treasure. The wardrobe and drawers were twisted and broken but I was excited and relieved as we pulled them out; but then sadness struck me. This was all that remained. This was all I possessed. We carried them to the post, which was to be my home for the next two months until I was able to get a place and bring my family together again.

At the time I did not think much of it but later when I settled down in my new home my thoughts wandered to my books, stamp collections and a rare and beautiful collection of post-cards and autographs of a grand selection of European celebrities in pre-war Europe. I was a keen Esperantist and I collected many small mementos from all over the world. Fellow Esperantists sent me autographs and stamps, some rare, some ordinary, but they all helped to build up a very picturesque collection which I treasured. The picture cards, especially as I had them catalogued, were very interesting and I often looked through them and went on an imaginary journey around the old romantic cities and villages of pre-war Europe.

The Nazis did not approve of the Esperanto movement and its idea of peace and brotherhood. Hundreds of Esperantists were executed or disappeared into concentration camps. I lost some personal friends in this way. I never met them but a close friendship had grown up between us as we wrote of our families, our hopes and dreams for the future. But that was before the war which was to shatter many hopes and dreams. Some of those who escaped imprisonment became involved in resistance movements and helped Jews and others escape arrest and certain death in concentration camps. They helped to organise escape routes using links they had with other Esperantists.

I made contact with some of these modest heroes after the war and was moved by their stories of privation and hardship. The stories, told in simple language, revealed many aspects of life in occupied Europe which the vast number of books published after the war failed to capture.

The corner of Antrim Road and Cranburn Street, 22 June, 1941.

Coulters were forced to transfer their business to the Cliftonville Road because of the damage inflicted during the Easter blitz. The author had been standing on the corner of Cranburn Street when the cluster of bombs hit the area. He and his companions dived behind the shelter and survived. (See page 41)

The ruins of the author's home in Cranburn Street were just around the corner, destroyed by the mine which fell on Lincoln Avenue. (See pages 30–1 and page 73)

9   Seven long days

I have already given some idea of the panic which compelled
100,000 people to flee from the city and the scenes which
accompanied this wild rush to put as much distance as possible between themselves and Belfast before nightfall. On
looking back and comparing the stories of hardship, loneliness
and the inability of those who left to adapt themselves to the
new style of life, it would be difficult to come to a firm
conclusion as to who suffered the most between those who left
and those who remained. One can only judge from the fact
that the majority decided to return to the city within the first
six weeks in spite of the threatened danger. For those who
remained, the rest of the week was a living nightmare. Above
all there was the nightly fear of the bombers returning, but
there were many other factors which added to the harshness of
the life style in the ghost town.

There were no milk or bread deliveries. Shopkeepers just
locked up their premises and went away to the safety of the
countryside. Water was unfit for use owing to pollution from
sewage. Army units brought water to distribution points and
the wardens helped to carry some to the old people. Those
who were fit were expected to bring their buckets and have
them filled at the mobile water trucks. Lavatories were not to
be used; instead residents were instructed to use buckets and
bury the contents. This was because of the damage done to
sewer pipes. Gas was used throughout the city as the means
for cooking and lighting but such was the damage to the mains
that it had to be turned off in the damaged areas, leaving the
unfortunate residents without lighting or cooking facilities.

Many chimneys were blocked by dislodged bricks and when
the fires were lit billowing clouds of smoke drove the choking

residents from their homes. We built some field kitchens for them and showed them how to dig shallow trenches and cover them with old grilles from windows. The fires were easy to feed and there was plenty of fuel to be found in the rubble. Buckets of water were soon boiling on these makeshift stoves. The people adapted themselves to this primitive way of life. Bread, milk and tinned food arrived at a feeding centre set up at the Holy Family church hall in Newington Avenue and we were able to get some supplies which we distributed. Every little thing we did was appreciated. These people who understood hardship and lived through hard times were like children trying to show their thanks. It is amazing what human beings can endure when they have the will to persevere. I observed this human endurance, and the ability to adapt, on many occasions during the week following the blitz.

Loneliness must have been a terrible experience especially during the night. In some streets there were only one or two families left. The streets were silent. The excited voices of the children as they skipped or played cowboys and indians in the narrow cobbled streets could no longer be heard. The children were all gone. Some were dead, killed in a horrible fashion before they had experienced life. Others were lucky and had survived and were now evacuated.

The loneliness did not only exist in the streets; the homes were stricken by it. Parents longed for the children they sent away to the safety of the countryside. Most of the children had never been away before except on a day trip organised by members of the local churches. Even on these rare occasions the anxious mothers waited at the railway station or church hall for their return. These few hours were the only experience of separation that families knew and now they were faced with only the name of some remote place to which their children had been evacuated.

Other inhabitants of the neighbourhood were also missed. 'It's awful. Even the pigeons have taken themselves off,' said one old fellow as I passed by. The locals loved the pigeons and made it a point of feeding them. The familiar scene of scores of pigeons sitting on the grey slated roofs or walking about leisurely on the cobbled streets pecking at pieces of food, was sorely missed. Feeding the pigeons came as naturally as feeding the family. The colony of pigeons in the area came about on account of a custom of the carters and dock labourers who brought home pockets full of corn and after they had their evening meal they would go out and feed the birds. I remember when I was a young boy an old docker used to share his corn with me and we would stand at his door and spread it. He liked to bring the birds right up to the door and they often walked over our feet as they fought greedily and gobbled up the corn we spread before them. Now the 'street hoakers' as we called them were not to be seen. The place had lost a part of its character; it was not the same without them.

Even in the most tragic circumstances the humour of the Belfast wits could still be found. Thank God for them. I always felt we needed them to brighten up dark moments. On one occasion there was a character who said 'Things are never so bad that they can't get worse.' Then there was another day when I went over to a chap who was standing staring at the ruins of his home. He looked at me and said 'I've often heard of jerry-builders but those fellows up there must have been jerry-wreckers.' The words evacuation and evacuated were new in the vocabulary of the locals and many clangers were dropped when they tried to use them. There was a woman one day whom I heard telling a shopkeeper that her children had been 'evaporated'.

Replacement of lost ration books always entailed much form filling and finally one had to have the form witnessed by a justice of the peace. One day an old lady who we were helping to fill in one of these forms came out with a whopper. 'That man Churchill, I think he said something about these ration books.' I looked at her inquiringly, 'What do you mean?' I asked. She was witty old dear and came back immediately. 'Did you never hear him say: Never was so much done by so many for so little?' I could see her point; she was hitting at the meagre ration allowance after all the trouble there was to go through to get a new book. Of course she was twisting the famous salute Churchill used to honour the R.A.F. 'Never was so much done for so many by so few.'

The work of the wardens was divided between rescue operations and welfare at the advice centres set up at the post. The rescue work in the initial stages created no special problems, apart from what appeared to be the impossible task of moving and searching the massive mounds of debris. The shortage of experienced volunteers in all the sections of the A.R.P. resulted in long and unrelieved spells of duty. Rescue operations were slow and here I must explain the difference between debris removal, which was carried out by gangs of workmen, and the search and clearance of debris, which was undertaken by teams of trained rescue workers. If our information led us to believe that bodies, or as we hoped living people, were buried under the mountains of debris, this debris had to be removed by hand and marked as having been searched. Large pieces of masonry and heavy beams were drawn out carefully or tunnelled under. Great care was necessary at this stage because it was possible to find people alive in cavities or voids as we called them. The voids were formed when beams and sections of flooring jammed and did not completely collapse, and many owe their lives to the understanding by the rescue teams of the principle of collapse. Never were the words of the old proverb so correct as when applied to rescue operations 'Fools rush in where wise men fear to tread.' Even walking carelessly over debris could cause a disaster. Only those who took part in rescue operations can describe the thrill and the overpowering emotions that gripped them as they crawled into a cavity and found someone still alive, even after several days.

Unfortunately, relatives who stood by anxiously did not understand that the rescue teams were skilled workers following well tested procedures. They became angry and complained that the rescue operations were taking too long. I dread to think what would have been the result in many cases where teams were successful in bringing out bodies alive if they had acted on the advice of the distraught relatives and used unorthodox methods to remove the debris quickly. The facts of all rescue operations were plain for everyone to see. Those who perished were either blown to pieces or crushed by falling buildings. Those who were rescued were saved by the skill and perseverance of the rescue men.

I will now return to the rescue operations after the air raid where we were personally involved, and the gruesome tasks we undertook. Owing to my knowledge and personal acquaintance with the people of the area I was called on several occasions to make positive identification of bodies recovered from the ruins. It was a heart breaking and sickening duty to perform, but in the circumstances it was expected that I would carry this burden of responsibility. During the years on patrol I made close friends with the residents and their children. Now I had to examine their mangled and decomposed bodies at close range in order to certify identification.

There was one black day I can remember well. It was the Friday following the raid, when the operations were coming to a close and bodies were being unearthed from beneath buried staircases and collapsed chimney breasts. I had just returned to the post after identifying a family of four when a warden came in and said 'I'm sorry, Jimmy, but they've found something in Lincoln Avenue that they would like you to look at.' This was the site of a disaster in which 15 people died and I expected another gruesome find and a further ordeal of identification. I was not wrong. The bodies were blown to pieces and I identified the family by the battered flaxen haired head of the little girl and a turned down fancy sock on the severed leg of her brother. As for the rest of the remains they were unrecognisable as human beings. There were several families involved in this incident and although we checked and rechecked the debris and immediate area there was a family of two which could not be accounted for. They must have been blown to pieces. Their deaths were confirmed later by a special court inquiry. This was the only case of its kind that arose from the blitz in Northern Ireland.

The rescue operations finally finished: the end of a grim week. It was a great relief to all those involved. Post 381 was faced with the most gruelling tasks not only in their own area but in those immediate post areas where organisation had broken down. Only those who took part in the last awful days of the rescue operations knew what it meant to be free from the nightmare duties that they had lived with during that momentous and horrific week.

Clearing up in Eglinton Street, 22 June, 1941. (Ulster Museum Garland Collection)
The lengthy process of salvage and of removing the debris from shattered homes continued for months. The old church and school were being used as an army billet at the time of the raid. The author had passed this scene when the damage was fresh, on his way to help at the mortuary at the Falls Road Baths. (See pages 50–1)

10 Welfare and the confidence tricksters

The rescue operations were finished but the wardens were still faced with a growing amount of welfare work and inquiries. They were responsible, as far as it was possible, for the identification of the homeless and others entitled to help from the welfare services, and they continued to issue homeless certificates and other documents.

There will always be scoundrels who will take advantage of any situation to advance their own selfish ends. Even the blitz with all its horrors and suffering was no exception to the rogues and the greedy. On the contrary, it was their intention, in the confusion that existed, to get as much as they could as quickly as possible. On our part we took the action of these leeches as a challenge and we used all our resourcefulness to thwart their plans. Trying to spot the rogues added a little colour to what was often a depressing spell of duty.

In the adjoining areas, organisation had broken down or the number of wardens on the ground was too small to operate any effective control. In these circumstances people of whom we had no knowledge were coming to our post seeking help. We sensed that some of them were frauds but there was little we could do but accept their stories. Re-organisation helped to fill the gap and the work really started in earnest.

Although we were the heaviest hit part of the city our organisation and administration held together and we still had the largest number of wardens operating in the district if not in the entire city. Headquarters asked our post to take over the immediate areas surrounding us or to lend some experienced wardens to posts whose numbers were severely depleted. Some of our wardens helped to man a new post set up to replace the ill-fated one in Trinity Street, where the group

warden and others were killed when the post was demolished
by a parachute mine. Norman Sharge took over the position of
post warden at Purdon Hall, an adjoining area to our own.
Norman was a member of the local Jewish community and he,
and other members of his people, played an important part
throughout the blitz and the follow-up operations. Another
member of this community and one of our wardens was Harry
Hyman, known to his friends as Midge. Harry was small in
stature but a giant with his spontaneous wit. He was a natural
comedian and was a tonic to us all during the long war years.

The Duncairn Gardens and Hillman Street area was severely
damaged and we took over control of the post. One of our
wardens took over administration and I incorporated it with
my operational duties. The new organisation resulted in a
tighter control in the wider area; this emergency reinforcing
forged links which bound the various posts together where
previously they had jealously guarded their own boundaries. I
can recall reading an article about civil defence volunteers in a
London borough bitterly complaining about wardens from an
adjoining area who extinguished incendiary bombs in what
they regarded as their patch. Apparently it was the only action
in that area and they resented the other group interfering with
their bombs. This was not a joke but a serious article and I
quote it as an example of how some groups regarded their
boundaries as sacrosanct.

Unlike the warring London wardens our plan of co-
operation helped to tackle the problem of the confidence
tricksters. We made a new census of the complete damaged
area and made notes, where possible, of the former tenants
and their present whereabouts. The information was used not
only to counter the frauds but was useful in helping genuine
cases of hardship. Apart from their fraudulent schemes the
tricksters generally created a scene. They understood the
welfare regulations and demanded their legal rights. Some of
the frauds were professionals, whereas the wardens were
amateurs trying to carry out a difficult job. It was fortunate that
they could only operate in the early period of the emergency
when an immediate grant was somewhat easier to obtain, but
as regulations tightened they disappeared from the scene.

A large number of enquirers were strangers who sought

information about missing relatives. In anticipation of this, we
collected all the information available when we made the new
survey of the neighbourhood. Lists were also compiled on the
day of the great exodus when we took note of forwarding
addresses. But there were many all over the city who just got
up and left without registering with any of the agencies set up
to handle evacuation.

The lists, however, were limited and we could not trace
everyone in the area. Anxious relatives came from the country
and as far as Scotland and England and we could feel and see
how shocked they were when we could not supply them with
a forwarding address. There were lists of the dead and seriously injured and at least we were able to assure them that
their friends were safe. As the days passed by, comprehensive
lists compiled by rest centres, evacuation offices, labour
exchanges and hospitals were distributed and displayed in
public places. These lists helped to fill the gaps and the work
became easier to handle and yet another impossible task came
to an end.

The city, however, remained a place of fear and rumour.
Thousands left their homes each night and slept in the open on
the slopes of Cavehill or on the plateau at Bellevue. This was
the nightly trek for the people from the north side of the city.
People from other parts moved out each night towards the
Divis mountains or Castlereagh hills. The 'trekers' or 'ditchers'
as they became known continued this nightly exercise for
months after the raids. The trekers became the source of jokes
and comedy sketches. The government, however, took a
serious view of the practice. It regarded the nightly evacuation
of the city as bad for morale. It also caused bad time-keeping
and a loss of production in the factories. Workers would not
work night-shifts. The government feared they were losing
their authority and that treking was an outward sign of discon-
tent and loss of trust. People were determined to see to their
own safety in spite of pleas to remain at home.

Rumours continued to plague the population. From time to
time they spread with alarming rapidity and as the old folk
would say 'They never lost anything in the telling.' For
example, two public notices that appeared in the local press
almost caused a panic. There was danger of an epidemic due to

the contamination of water and other health hazards such as ruptured sewerage pipes from which sewage gushed over the streets. Animals including horses were killed during the raid and their carcasses remained in demolished stables or on the rubbish strewn streets for some time. Foodstuffs from damaged shops and premises lay rotting among the sewage. As a precautionary measure the health department set up immunisation centres. In a city already gripped by fear, the reaction to this measure almost created a complete panic. Rumours spread, especially in severely damaged areas, about outbreaks of cholera, dysentery and typhoid. This caused serious upset through the city. The wardens' posts were inundated with inquiries. Anxious mothers with children prepared to leave. The terror of the bombing had failed to break their spirits but the fear of a dreaded disease was mixed with folklore stories of an epidemic which hit the city many years ago when, nearby on the site of the first Royal Victoria Hospital in Frederick Street, hundreds of dead and dying were left outside on the street, as there was no room in the hospital to shelter them. The wardens did their best to allay their fears and in this respect we were successful. Our wardens were trusted and respected in the community especially after the blitz. The people brought us all their troubles and sought our advice. This was how we, and not the local doctors, became involved in this dramatic situation. It must be understood that working class families of fifty years ago did not have the opportunities in education that we have today. Many of them were illiterate and accepted rumours as fact, no matter how fantastic they may have appeared to others. It was difficult to convince them that there were no serious reports of any outbreaks of disease in the city. We pointed out that we also were part of the community and that we were in no way better protected than they were and advised them to go and be immunised as a precaution. Our advice was taken and the panic subsided, but with conditions as they were, we knew it would not be long before a new rumour would be born. We had not long to wait.

The announcement that 33 dangerous animals were to be destroyed at the Bellevue Zoo was the source of a new spate of rumours. The lions, tigers and other dangerous animals would have been an added threat to the public if they managed to escape in the event of another raid. The measure was purely precautionary but it gave rise to the rumour that the government had some information that another attack on the city was imminent. The rumour was more difficult to kill because we all believed in our hearts that there would be another attack on the city. It certainly increased the number of trekers and in this undefended city it was at the same time upsetting and yet comforting to see the populace leave each night in search of safety in the nearby hills. We agreed with their simple philosophy that danger was near but it did not take the shooting of some dangerous animals to convince us that they were right in their assumption.

This was the pattern of life at the time. Rumour followed rumour and nightfall brought fear. But gradually, and perhaps not so obviously, some kind of normality was creeping back into the city. Welfare services continued to attend to the homeless and the hundreds of problems that followed in the wake of the disaster. The other services carried on with the restoration of utility services and public transport and the demolition of dangerous buildings and the clearing of ugly sites of destruction.

How living conditions were ever restored to the north side of the city will forever remain a mystery, even to those who took part in the massive emergency operation. The north side suffered a tremendous amount of damage. Every building and house showed signs of the attack. Water and sewerage mains were extensively destroyed. Overhead wires and tram tracks were shattered. Electricity and gas mains and telephone cables, including the main trunk lines, also suffered. The death toll was staggering and as the work of clearing up continued new dangers in the form of a large number of unexploded bombs (U.X.Bs) were discovered.

Salisbury Avenue (Antrim Road) tram depot after the Easter air raid, 1941.

(Ludgate Collection)

This scene typifies the disruption to the everyday services in the North Belfast area.

11 Parachute mines and unexploded bombs

Parachute mines were sea mines adapted for carrying in aircraft. The use of these weapons gave the enemy a bomb, heavier and more powerful than anything previously employed. They were dropped from a great height and any wind could affect them and take them away from military and towards civilian targets. Damage was always severe and resulted in a heavy loss of life. Surface shelters offered little resistance or protection, and only in deep underground shelters could any degree of safety be expected.

During the Easter raids on Belfast a large number of these mines, intended for the port facilities, the shipbuilding and aircraft industry, came down in residential areas in the north of the city. What this meant in terms of human misery I have tried to explain. Row upon row of little dwelling houses collapsed leaving mountains of debris at which wardens dug and clawed with their bare hands in the hope of finding someone alive.

Unlike London, Belfast had no deep shelters and surface shelters were totally inadequate. Many stories are told and memories still remain of the terrible carnage that resulted when crowded shelters collapsed, killing all who sought refuge in them. In other incidents there were many stories of miraculous escapes but how could it be otherwise when the difference between life and death depended on the strength and direction of the wind as the silk parachutes floated gracefully to earth?

Experts give an explanation for the heavy blitzing of the Antrim Road area. They believe that the bombers mistook the waterworks reservoirs for the docks or some form of naval base. Several mines which did not explode were dropped into the waterworks and I will tell of these in more detail when I come to discuss the problems of unexploded bombs.

The unexploded bomb was not in all cases due to a faulty fuse but was sometimes designed deliberately as a strategic weapon. It was used on railway tracks, marshalling yards, airfields and in the vicinity of factories. In this respect it was a most effective weapon, causing confusion and disruption to production. In England hundreds of these bombs lay scattered across the country. Factories, marshalling yards and large sections of railway tracks could not be used. This was the effect that the enemy anticipated and it created problems that had to be tackled with all urgency to prevent transport and production grinding to a stop. The answer lay with a unit known as the bomb disposal squad or B.D.S.'s as they were generally called. The work carried out by these men was little short of suicide. Their job was to render these bombs safe. Without modern equipment as we know it today such as X-rays, television and other technical gear the men of the B.D.S. bought experience with their lives. Some of them had a long run, others but a short one. However, whether it was their twentieth or their first the bomb disposal squad knew that, perhaps, the next assignment could be their last. In spite of the experience they were gaining, the work became more and more dangerous. The enemy understood that the bombs were being rendered harmless and they started to make them more dangerous and difficult to handle. They incorporated fuses of the most ingenious designs. They varied the type of fusing and in some cases several devices were fitted into bombs. The battle of the U.X.B.'s was being gradually won but every scrap of experience was paid for with human life and even with hard won experience the slaughter went on.

Belfast also had problems with the U.X.B.'s. Unlike other situations, control had to follow laid down guidelines to prevent disruption. Reports on U.X.B.'s came from various sources. Bombs sometimes could be sighted protruding from holes in the ground or wedged in the roof or floor of some building. This was by far the most dramatic and easiest way of identifying bombs. They were not always as easy as this. Most bombs were identified by statistical data and trustworthy information. There were reports of bombs being heard coming down but no signs of explosions. Teams of specially trained personnel known as bomb identification officers, B.I.O.'s, investigated these reports taking special note of the type and extent of damage to surrounding buildings. They tried to estimate the size of bomb from tail fins or collars. Craters or points of entry were examined for signs of explosion, pieces of shrapnel or fins pocked with holes made by flying shrapnel. Their completed reports were sent to B.D.S. control who decided on what action should be taken. In spite of this investigation the presence of a U.X.B. was still difficult to confirm in a devastated built-up area. Large U.X.B.'s could tear the front out of buildings and cause damage to windows in the vicinity. Sometimes they left small or large craters and even left large cracks on walls. It was the duty of the B.I.O.'s thoroughly to investigate every scrap of information. It was essential that every piece of knowledge was properly assessed, as wrong conclusions could lead to a U.X.B. being mistaken for one that had exploded.

During these preliminary investigations wardens were placed in a peculiar situation. They could not act impulsively and try to evacuate an area. At any rate the residents were reluctant to leave their homes, even when it was decided that evacuation was necessary. On the other hand if the B.D.S. confirmed a suspect device, we could only anticipate what emergency steps would have to be taken. Schools or church halls were earmarked and tentative arrangements made for their use if the necessity should arise. Estimates were made of the area of danger and the number that would be involved if evacuation was ordered. Of course, every U.X.B. operation had its own problems and the wardens had to work in close collaboration with the B.D.S. It will be appreciated that the services of the bomb squad were at a premium. There was not a permanent squad in Northern Ireland and the bomb squads employed after the blitz arrived from Britain. In fact there were two distinct squads who dealt with bombs. Naval units dealt with sea mines and certain parachute mines. They were known as bomb safety officers.

A complicated and near tragic incident occurred at a small block of shops. A U.X.B. was confirmed and the necessary evacuation was carried out. The B.D.S. made the bomb safe

and the area was declared clear. Then came a strange twist in
the affair. By chance there were two U.X.B.'s in the same
block. The other undetected one exploded later and wrecked
the block of shops. There were some casualties but fortunately
no one was seriously hurt.

On one occasion a large bomb was discovered just behind
the perimeter wall of the Victoria Barracks. This was the wall
that ran behind the houses in Lepper Street which was a
thickly populated part of our area. If this bomb had exploded
when it fell the casualty figures could have certainly been high.

The bomb squad decided that the bomb was too dangerous
to work with and that it would have to be exploded on the site.
Thick sandbag walls were built around it and hundreds of
sandbags were placed on top. Arrangements were made to
explode the bomb at 3 p.m. that day. The police drove around
the designated area calling on residents to leave their homes
and to keep their doors and windows open. The wardens
made a personal check of each dwelling to make sure that no
one remained in the houses. The area was sealed off and we
retired to a safe distance and waited.

As usual no matter how tense the situation was the wits
always added a bit of colour to the affair. One character said 'I
was reading about one of these bomb fellows. He was down a
hole working at one of them bombs when he started shouting
to be pulled out. His mates rushed forward and dragged him
out. They ran back for about 50 yards pulling him with them
and threw themselves on the ground. Nothing happened.
They looked enquiringly at their companion. He was seriously
upset, pale and breathless. "My God," he said, "You should
have seen the size of that rat down there".'

Some more stories were exchanged while we waited. The
seconds and then the minutes went by. Then it happened.
There was a terrific explosion and even at a distance we could
feel the air pressure. From our vantage point we could see torn
sandbags rising in the air. Slates and glass scattered on the
pavement and a great cloud of smoke and dust hung over the
area. It was amazing to stand and watch the effects of the
explosion. This was the only U.X.B. in Belfast that was dealt
with in this way. For those who watched the operation it was a
unique experience.

The largest U.X.B. operation did not come at this time, but some years later. It was generally believed that there were a number of U.X.B.'s in the waterworks but no attempt was made to clear them. A number of unexploded missiles similar to those suspected of being in the waterworks exploded in Britain after a long delay and caused several deaths. After this it was decided to investigate the missiles in the waterworks.

The waterworks, a large open park and pleasure garden, was not in our post area. But very little went on in civil defence, social or operational, in which Post 381 did not play a part. Accordingly, we were asked to help and I left with six of our wardens to report to the post at Kelvin Parade, which was being used as the headquarters for the operation. Owing to the large number of nearby houses and the crowds that fre-quented the park, the clearance was given priority and an experienced team arrived from England. The operation was considered dangerous. The suspect missiles were parachute mines and according to intelligence reports they were fitted with anti-handling and pressure devices and possibly a few more booby traps. There were several mines to deal with and it was expected that the operation would take a few days to complete. There was no doubt as to the destructive power of mines and a strict evacuation of the area defined by the B.D.S. was carried out.

The operation started on a Sunday afternoon and continued until about 4 p.m. on Monday. Police and wardens helped with the evacuation. It was just like a scene from the blitz all over again. There was no fear or panic but they came along carrying suitcases and parcels. Some had bird cages and children never seemed to forget their toys. When the evacu-ation was complete, the area was roped off and signs were displayed:

DANGER   U.X.B.   KEEP OUT

The wardens patrolled the area and made sure that no one entered the danger zone. The police joined us on these patrols and used their authority to enforce the no entry regulations. A church hall nearby was used as a centre but later in the night some people tried to return to their homes and they had to be turned back. Young people were the worst offenders: they climbed into the waterworks and made their way home unnoticed.

It was a cold night but we were able to go to the post for a short rest and some refreshments. The good ladies of the civil defence and the W.V.S. never failed to turn up with their tea pot. In fact the ladies and their tea became a bit of a joke in civil defence circles but I can assure those ladies, and there are still some around, that to the wardens who kept many all night vigils, their cups of tea and sandwiches were greatly appreciated.

Morning came and anxious crowds began to gather and we had to turn down all requests for permission to visit their homes. Some just wanted to see if they had closed their doors before they left. Others wanted to go and find their cats or dogs which were not at home when they left. Their anxiety for their pets and houses was understandable but with the operation at the most dangerous stage it was certainly not the time to let them pass. As the day progressed the appeals and attempts to get through became more persistent. People did not realise the dangerous state of the bombs and that the men in the park were gambling with their lives. In fact the B.D.S. officer in charge of the operation was blown to pieces a few weeks later while working elsewhere on a similar type bomb. When word came through of his death it hit me like the loss of a personal friend. I had only seen him twice but it is hard to forget the face of a brave man.

It was well into the day when the all clear notice came. The ropes and warning notices came down. It was time to go home.

12   The fire blitz: May 4/5 1941

The wardens continued to deal with the everyday problems that arose in their neighbourhood and at the same time, together with the A.R.P. services as a whole, to prepare for the possibility of another attack. German intelligence reports must have shown that although the Easter raid had caused considerable damage, their objective, namely the destruction of the port facilities and shipyards, had not been achieved. Belfast port facilities, shipyards and aircraft production were of strategic value in the war effort and in all probability another raid on the city would be planned. With these thoughts in mind every effort was made to find new recruits and in the light of experience further plans were made to meet another attack if it should come. It was a race against time. Little did we know that a fresh disaster was just around the corner.

For the second time in a few weeks the sirens wailed out the warning that enemy aircraft were approaching the city. All the dreadful memories of the previous raid came flashing to mind as the silence of the night was broken. I was on patrol with a group of wardens when the alert was sounded. We had kept up these nightly patrols since Easter partly in order to keep in touch with the people in the lonely streets. The early contact we made with the residents and the few words of advice we gave them as we hurried back to the post helped to produce some element of calm which remained in spite of the terror of the night.

Again I must emphasise how pitiful and distressing the situation was for those people. For weeks they had lived primitively in an area that remained a shambles. In many of the little streets only a few families remained and now they were about to face another lonely night of terror. We knew that they put great trust in us but all that we could do as we left them was to promise that we would be back.

At the post there was much excitement and activity. The duty room was crowded as the patrolling wardens returned to be briefed on their duties. Wardens who had been at home made their way to the post and gradually our strength mounted. The final check revealed a full muster, around thirty to cover the four sectors. Post 381 had stood the test in spite of the horrors of the previous raid. I had a wonderful feeling of security in knowing that I would be working with this great bunch of men. They knew the danger but here they were again ready to serve their community. Each senior warden briefed his own team as we prepared to move out. Our equipment consisted of stirrup pumps, buckets, ropes, axes and a stretcher with two blankets for each team. The standard of equipment had not improved but at least there was now sufficient to go around.

Thus equipped we moved out in a confident but serious mood with each man knowing that he might again be called upon to act as doctor, fireman, rescuer and counsellor. Previous experience had proved that our forecast of heavy damage in the barracks area was correct and our strategy was to cover these streets in as far as our numbers would permit. There was also the obligation of keeping in contact with those terrified and lonely residents who were spread throughout the whole area. We had the added responsibility for covering the adjoining areas which we had been asked to take over. I was in charge of this combined operation, although I had no extra volunteers. The combined area consisted of my own sector and a complete post area around Hillman Street. Unfortunately the discipline broke down there and they were left with only a few willing volunteers.

The new territory was similar to our own with a slightly roomier, stronger built type of dwelling. The joint plan of operation had some advantages. Although it stretched the wardens out further on the ground it did give us the facilities of the Hillman Street School. In the Easter raid our wardens had to operate entirely in the open, isolated from their post and cut off from communication. Working within this new set-up there was a chance of telephone communication and good cover to treat casualties if necessary and, of course, one of our wardens was in charge of administration as post warden.

The area was a warren of little streets with tightly packed back-to-back houses. One mine was sufficient to tear away two or three streets and fires, as we knew, would be difficult to contain. Water mains were only temporarily repaired and much equipment was damaged in the previous raids. Civil defence strength was lower over the whole of the city and the remaining volunteers faced a sterner test than before. The whole situation seemed impossible. However, the people decided to stay and we had promised to be with them and this we intended to do.

The wardens were thin on the ground and although I was concentrating on what was believed to be the most vulnerable part, other wardens were spread out over the rest of the post area. This was the setting in which we waited for another onslaught on the district. The raid developed quickly. It was not long until the sounds of explosions could be heard coming from the city centre. This time the bombers were finding their targets quickly. The noise of exploding bombs and heavy drone of loaded planes came nearer. The guns in the barracks broke the silence with a thunderous barrage as they pumped anti-aircraft shells into the blackness of the night. The little houses shook as the guns kept up their constant fire. Shrapnel from bursting shells fell like rain and large pieces came crashing down on rooftops and roadways. The sound of the explosions became more distinct as the Clifton Street side of the barracks came under attack. The guns thundered again, this time more furiously as they put up a barrage in an attempt to drive away the advancing planes.

It was lonely and frightening as I walked alone through the small dark streets and listened to the thunder of the guns. The noise was terrific as it became trapped in the narrow streets. It seemed to reverberate off the walls and the very ground shook with vibrations. For distraction I kept looking at the sky, which was ablaze with anti-aircraft shells as they burst into balls of fire. Soon the city centre was burning fiercely and the flames were reflected in the sky like an ocean of fire. Loud rumblings filled the air as roofs collapsed and showers of sparks shot up into the air like an erupting volcano. To keep myself occupied as I moved along I tried to picture just which buildings were burning. It was a useless exercise but it helped to break the tension at the time.

My companions were scattered about in small groups. I knew their mettle and had no doubt I could depend on them if anything came our way that night. Nevertheless, it was a particularly dangerous area and I felt responsible in some way for them. I decided to make a quick patrol around the whole sector and see where they had positioned themselves. The first one I met was my old mate Montague. He was glad to see me. 'I was hoping to see you,' he said. 'Don't worry,' I replied. 'I'll join up with you later. I'm just having a walk around to see that everyone is all right. I kind of became anxious about them.' He joined me and we moved around. It was my plan that should anything happen we would join up as a team and do what we could. In the meantime the wardens were on patrol, watching.

Suddenly there was a change in the sound of the planes as they flew overhead. They appeared to be flying faster and at a lower altitude. The area was again under attack. Hundreds of silver-like cylindrical objects came down like rain from the sky. They crashed through roofs and windows. Incendiary bombs were used in the previous raid but not on the same scale. Widespread fire in an area such as this was a frightening thought and I recalled reading about a raid on London in which the Germans almost exclusively used incendiary bombs, with devastating results.

These small bombs weighed 1 kilo and so they were known as kilo bombs. The British and Americans used a heavier type, about twice that of the German standard model. This heavier bomb, used by the Allies, was capable of greater penetration and proved a better weapon where roofs were reinforced. The Germans used a variety of incendiary weapons but they never abandoned the use of the kilo bomb.

These bombs, which exploded and sent pieces of burning magnesium flying in all directions, were very effective, especially when dropped in large quantities, and when left unattended could cause more damage than a high explosive bomb which cost hundreds of pounds to produce.

As planned, our flying squad again came into action and the other wardens continued to act as our eyes and ears. Dozens of incendiaries were burning in the roadway. We were taught to cover these bombs with sand or to place a sandbag gently on top of them. With hundreds of the bombs falling all around this was another piece of useless textbook information. We did not have the men or the time and at any rate they could do no harm so we left them to burn. However, not all of them went astray. Several houses were blazing and fires were just starting in others as each new lot of bombs came raining down. The city was ablaze. The fire service was being hard pressed. Every available pump was in action and urgent appeals for rein-forcements went out to other regions. With the exception of a few auxiliary fire service trailer pumps which moved around the whole district, we were left again to face another onslaught virtually on our own.

At times miracles do seem to happen: how else can certain things be explained? Something like a miracle happened that night. To our amazement the locals who had lived in fear and near panic during the previous weeks came out and were prepared to help us. The men turned up with sledgehammers and axes. The women, freed from the anxiety of looking after their children's safety, also lent a hand and carried buckets of water. The extra help was a great boost not only in numbers but also for our morale. I took advantage of the new situation and spread my wardens out further and used them to direct the work of the civilian firefighters.

It was not realised at the time but we were witnessing the start of a new section in civil defence which was to develop in two stages. The first of these were the street fire parties, later to be merged into a more efficient body to be known as the fireguards. I will describe this body and its training and organisation in a later chapter.

The unexpected help left me free to guide and supervise the whole operation. I moved about quickly from street to street. The guns were still thundering but there was little time to take notice of them or the falling shrapnel. The excitement of the battle certainly drove us on. There was so much to do and we could see the growing fires just as they happened, and above us the glowing flames reflected in the sky told us we were not alone in being on the receiving end of the enemy attack.

Where it was possible, fires were tackled immediately before they could get a good hold. Beds in many cases were at the heart of the fire and the quickest way to tackle this sort of fire was to bundle up the mattress or bedclothes and throw them out of the window. Speed and quick decisions were the key to success. The old houses were like tinder boxes and there were a few narrow escapes when fires suddenly got out of control. Unlike professional firemen, we were amateurs and did not always appreciate the dangers of fire spread. Furthermore our equipment forced us to go closer to fires than we would have wished. I now found myself having to make decisions on whether we should attempt to go into certain buildings. It was a difficult and painful duty to have to make such decisions but the safety of my men, especially when there was no question of life saving, had to come first. Some of the civilian firefighters were faced with accepting my decisions or risking their lives in a vain attempt to save their own or a friend's home. The old houses offered no resistance to the hungry flames that engulfed them in a matter of minutes. In cases where we had to withdraw, all we could do was to snatch at some piece of furniture, a cherished ornament or picture.

I could not help but marvel at the enthusiasm and self-sacrifice of these volunteers. War has an impact on human character. It makes heroes out of quiet fellows and I witnessed this change of personality in people as they threw their whole weight into their efforts to control the fires. Even their appreciation of dangerous situations came naturally to them and I was happy that I did not have to make many more decisions.

It was pathetic to see people watch their homes burn. Many of them were born in the houses as were their parents before them. It was not only their homes that they stood watching as the flames engulfed them. With the destruction of their houses went all the scenes of their childhood and the memories of growing up.

So far no high explosive bombs had fallen in the area and we were able at least to fight the fires without that added danger. There were few people left and the carnage we had experienced before would not happen again. Most of the remaining residents were with us and the older ones were in the shelters and we kept an eye on them from time to time. This is how we operated throughout the night. We won some and we lost some, but as one of the fellows said, 'you can't win them all.' One of those buildings lost was a school. In this incident we were on the losing side from the start. We did not have the equipment for fighting large fires. The school was of an old type with plenty of timber and books to feed the flames that crept from room to room. The school catered for a large section of the neighbourhood and its loss caused difficulties when the district came back to some degree of normality.

Of all the fires we met, there is one which must remain as one of my special memories. I had just returned from the post in Hillman Street and we were on the move looking for fires we thought we could control. One of the wardens on patrol brought us word on a fire at a house in which there was a wake. This was one we would have to win. I chose a few experienced wardens and some helpers and set off with our stirrup pumps and buckets. When we arrived at the house, the family was in distress and the mourners who continued to pray were clearly disturbed, not knowing what to do. The corpse was laid out and candles were burning on a table beside the coffin. As we came to the house the fire was still confined to the roof-space so we rushed up the stairs to investigate. An incendiary bomb had crashed through the roof and was wedged in the rafters. There was no trap door to the roof-space and we had no ladders to tackle it from the outside. I decided to hack a hole in the ceiling with my axe. There was a heavy set of Scotch drawers in the room. I pulled them to the centre of the room and scrambled up on them. They were a good height and they supported my weight as I hacked at the ceiling and cut a fair sized hole. The stirrup pump team came prancing up the stairs with buckets of water and pumps. From my position on top of the drawers I was then able to extinguish the fire before it got a chance of spreading. The team kept up a strong flow of water and I soaked and raked the embers to prevent them from re-kindling. I was so engrossed with what I was doing that I did not notice that some burning embers had dropped on my back and that my coat was smouldering. One of the wardens shouted to me 'Jimmy, your coat's on fire'. I pulled it off before it burned through to my skin and threw it down to them to stamp it out. At last I shouted somewhat triumphantly 'Water off' and the team laughed. They knew they had won a special kind of victory.

All faces turned to us as we made our way down the stairs. The prayers which we could hear as we were fighting the fire stopped as we came into the room. We assured them that the fire was out but that there would be some cleaning up to do. As we left to join our comrades the mourners called for God's blessing on us and we could hear the renewed bursts of prayers which we guessed were for our benefit as we moved off into the darkness. For a long time afterwards we were referred to as the squad who rescued a corpse.

The guns kept up their barrage and in the warren of little streets the noise was deafening. I am sure we got the vibrations of the guns more than the crews who were actually using them. However, it was good to hear them and to know that the planes were meeting with some opposition no matter how ineffective it was. I could remember the deep feeling of despair that gripped the civil defence workers on Easter Tuesday when they realised there was no defence against the planes that flew about at will in the clouds above them. It had been sickening to know that we stood alone.

The element of surprise that caught the city unprepared did not operate this time or create such a panic. Certainly more than half the city had left and thousands more were in the surrounding hills but many were determined to remain. It was some of these people who joined our meagre bunch of wardens and helped to fight the fires even in the houses of those who went away.

In the built-up areas, it was left to the local wardens to co-ordinate any assistance that came to their aid. Fire was everywhere. The little houses burned out quickly and as I watched the last flickering flames light up the dark holes that were once the doors and windows I could not help but compare the burned out dwellings with the lantern turnips which children carry at Hallow'een with flickering candles inside throwing flashes of light through the cut out holes.

Meanwhile, great fires were raging in the dockland area and flames and smoke could be seen whirling and spiralling towards the sky. As we tried to control the small fires in the tiny houses we could not but think of the magnitude of the task facing the firemen in that sea of fire. Nearby, the York Street Mill was once more the target of the bombers. Emergency repairs had been carried out after the Easter raid and full production was planned for Monday when the mill was to be reopened. However, the mill was doomed and in a few hours all that remained of it was a giant mass of rubble.

The scene was spectacular. The largest mill of its kind in the world was blazing from end to end. I could not keep my eyes off it as I stood hypnotised by the magnitude and power of the inferno. It was the largest fire ever seen in the city. The factory stood on an island, a massive six storey building covering a space of 100 yards by 300 yards. What a sight it was. Flames licked hungrily around the building as they burst through the hundreds of little windows on each floor. Showers of sparks and flames leapt to the sky as sections of the roof collapsed. The sparks came fluttering down like a snowstorm. They irritated my hands and face as they descended. The ground shook as floors collapsed and the heavy machinery went crashing down into the rooms below. The air became intolerably warm and at times it felt like being in a furnace as the flames burst afresh through each new opening. The intense heat became trapped in the network of little streets opposite the mill in Henry Street. The wardens from Great Georges Street post were busy in these streets persuading the residents to move out into Great Georges Street. The temperature had reached such heights, it was feared that the houses would burst into flames. The wardens called on the firemen to play their hoses into the area. The firemen, who were driven back by the heat, now concentrated for a few minutes on trying to reduce the temperature in the warren of little streets. Steam rose from the hot roofs as the spray from the hoses hit them. They doused the houses and played their hoses into the air and brought down the temperature so that it became tolerable to relax for a few moments before returning to the inferno just around the corner.

The speed with which the fire was devouring the building was amazing. The sound of crashing machinery continued as the supporting structures collapsed and walls began to crumble and collapse. I could have watched for the rest of the night. As there were no casualties or loss of life the incident was not so upsetting as others we had witnessed. For me watching the fire was another unforgettable memory in a long calendar of events. Elsewhere, however, there was work more suitable to our meagre equipment.

Belfast was proud of its flax spinning mill but that night there were few present to witness the last hours of this historic building which marked the part the city played in the great industrial revolution.

Apart from the blazing inferno at the mill, fires were raging everywhere. In the city centre firemen fought a losing battle with the growing fires. They did not have the manpower or the equipment which the fire situation demanded. Every available pump and hose was pressed into action but at the height of the operation the water pressure dropped. The hoses went dry. The battle was lost. There were 70 major ruptures of water mains compared with 37 during the previous raids: high explosives were used as well as incendiaries. No provision had been made for emergency water supplies. This was done later but tomorrow is always too late. The firemen could only stand and watch or damp down adjoining buildings with the weak trickles of water that remained.

The taste and smell of smoke was heavy in the air as I moved about on a sightseeing tour of the city in the early hours of the morning. Smouldering buildings and the burned-out frames of what had been fashionable stores and offices told their own frightening story of the fire blitz on Belfast. Water sprayed like fountains from damaged fire hoses. Smoke begrimed and tired firemen continued to damp down buildings or to contain fires that still were burning in the larger blocks.

'How and when could the Belfast I knew ever return?' I asked myself as I trudged through pools of water and stepped over the tangled hoses that lay scattered all around me.

Belfast had been the target for a fire blitz. This was a new strategy in aerial warfare. The first phase of the operation was carried out by planes dropping high explosive bombs. Then followed waves of planes which dropped thousands of incendiary bombs into the target area. At the height of the fires the bombers returned and dropped more bombs. This was to open up more buildings and to force the firefighters to take cover and thus to permit the fires to spread and get out of control.

It was the fire blitz that beat civil defence workers everywhere, let it be in London, Belfast, Tokyo, Hamburg or other German cities. It was fire bombing that destroyed Hamburg in a single raid. The fires joined up and caused a fire storm which raged through the city and killed 80,000.

London experienced two big fire raids. The first was in 1940 and a few nights after the raid on Belfast the bombers returned to London and delivered what was one of the most severe raids of the war. The Thames was at low tide, a fact no doubt allowed for in the timing of the attack. In the course of the night the water supply failed and London firemen had to stand as our men had stood and watch their city burn.

I have another vivid memory of the Belfast incendiary raid which at times makes me go a little cold all over, especially when I think of how stupid I had been. During the night the wardens picked up pieces of shrapnel, tail fins, collars and such like things for souvenirs. Unexploded incendiary bombs were plentiful and could be picked up everywhere. The I.B.'s as they were known were reasonably safe to handle and were regarded as good souvenirs. I found one that was slightly different in length and appearance. I did not see anything like it during the night nor had I seen any pictures of it. I knew the Germans produced several types of incendiary bombs and I believed that this was one of them. I did not wish to lose it and I carried it about with me throughout the night. I hid it while I worked and retrieved it again as I moved on.

The next morning we produced our souvenirs. There was the usual lot but one fellow proudly produced an incendiary bomb container. These special containers were used to ensure close distribution of the incendiaries. They resembled a small bin and were primed to explode and burst open at a predetermined height after they left the plane. The incendiaries came tumbling out and the container hurtled down to earth. This particular one fell into the backyard of one of the local residents. The next morning she discovered it in her yard and came to the post rather frightened and excited. John recognised it and with great enthusiasm he took it away. It was certainly the prize of the night.

When I produced my bomb it attracted plenty of attention. It was examined carefully and luckily we did not attempt to dismantle it as we had done with ordinary incendiaries. It was treated with a certain amount of respect and placed in a sandbag trench specially built at the back of the post for storing any suspicious articles found after a raid. A report on it was made out and sent to district headquarters. Later on in the day a general message from headquarters was circulated warning wardens to be on the look-out for unusual looking incendiary bombs. The message went on to say that they contained an explosive charge which made it an anti-personnel bomb as well as an incendiary agent. The bombs were to be handled carefully and the police were to be notified.

As I read the message a tremor passed through me. I realised I had gambled with death and won.

The district had received another pounding but, with the exception of one incident, the casualty list was small. The Glenravel Street Police Station received a direct hit, killing five young recruits just out of the depot and a police sergeant also recently transferred after having served 23 years in his previous station.

However, it was the east side of the city which had been the main target for the bombers. Shipyards, aircraft factories and port facilities came under heavy attack. Reports from German crews who flew over in waves tell how they could see the vast conflagrations as they approached the city even from many miles away from the target area. Production in the industrial area, already as low as 25% due to absenteeism, fell far lower and it was almost a year before near full production was attained.

Casualty figures, however, were a fraction of those incurred during previous raids and were in the region of about 150 killed. The earlier massive evacuation and the fact that wardens were able to encourage people to seek shelter and not to remain in their little houses in the east and north side of the city was responsible for the dramatic drop in casualties.

Wardens' posts were again used as advice centres. In our own case there were not the same frantic crowds. However, the raid resulted in a further loss of dwellings and this brought new problems just as complex as we had to deal with previously. The problem we now had to face was that the locals did not want to leave. In spite of all they had suffered in the two raids and the destruction of their homes, they wished to remain in the neighbourhood they loved and of which they were a part.

Emergency repairs to houses did not come under the control of the wardens but where houses were only partly damaged we did our best to have repairs carried out. Accommodation even before the blitz was inadequate and overcrowding was a common complaint throughout the entire locality and the bombing added greatly to existing social problems. There was nothing to be done for the homeless but to refer them to the welfare authorities in order to obtain some form of accommodation elsewhere. At a later stage, special legislation empowered the Ministry for Public Security to transfer the tenancies of dwelling houses where tenants had completely abandoned them, without any notice of their intention of returning to them being made to the landlords. This eased the situation, although it caused unpleasantness and rows when former tenants decided to return to the city. The new tenants were not squatters but legal tenants protected by law.

After the fire blitz of 4/5 May 1941 another evacuation took place. This time, however, it was more orderly and there were not the same spectacular scenes as when 100,000 fearful and panic driven people tried to flee the city. The wild scenes at the bus and railway stations were not repeated. The transport authorities had sufficient facilities to handle the emergency.

Many of those who left the city did not return. Some settled in their adopted surroundings and others emigrated after the war.

York Street Mill, 20 June, 1941.   (Ulster Museum Garland Collection)
*These pictures, taken after the embers had cooled, can give only an impression of the fury
of the fire blitz which the author had watched. (See pages 95–6)*

13   The passing of an era

The bombs and the fires changed and destroyed a way of life in which the local communities had grown up. Most of the residents and their parents before them were born in the area and now they were reluctant to leave. The old areas were steeped in folklore and tradition and the locals feared that they would be lost and strangers in any environment other than their own. The life of the community could be traced in the folklore that surrounded a spinning mill, a church, pawn-shops, a few picture houses and a large public house and billiard hall.

The mill was the centre of the lifestyle of the local community, although many from outside the immediate area might work there. Among the older residents were those who had worked in the mill as halftimers. This was a system in which young children aged between 9 years and 12 years went to school for three days and went to work at the mill for the other three, from 6 o'clock in the morning till 6 at night including Saturdays. It was hard work for a child but they accepted it as the only kind of life they knew and understood. Besides being strenuous, the conditions were unhygienic and at times the children were brutally treated by those placed in charge of them. It was amazing that people with such memories wanted to remain in the district when they were offered a chance to leave. To me it was wonderful at the time that people who acted a leading part in this grim period of the social history of Belfast were still amongst us.

For generations the mill was the sole means of support for the people of the district. During the depression years of the 1920s and 30s it was the women in the mill who supported their families when the men could not find work. The York

Street spinning factory was the largest of its kind in the world
and its destruction led to many economic problems in an
already deprived and run down area. The war as yet had not
brought full employment to Northern Ireland and the mill was
one of the few factories which was working at full capacity.
The hardship caused by its destruction is one of the untold
stories of the blitz.

With its passing went the familiar early morning scene of
dozens of girls and women, some of them wearing men's
boots, moving along through the narrow streets with arms
linked and singing at the top of their voices the well known
mill songs or parodies based on the popular songs of the day.
The crowd grew as the workers coming from different directions converged on the mill and as they reached the gates their
voices rose to a crescendo which echoed and re-echoed in the
narrow streets surrounding the mill. The parodies were amusing and impromptu and generally referred in a not too bene-
volent fashion to some member of the lower managerial staff,
local politicians or councillors. Well-known characters from
time to time because the targets of the poetic wits among the
mill workers. This was the traditional ritual practised by the
women each morning and evening as they made their way to
and from the factory.

Silent streets now greeted the wardens as they went on their
early morning patrols. On those dark mornings at times I
imagined or expected to hear or see a group of chanting girls
emerge from the darkness. The passing of the mill removed
many colourful characters from the scene. Yes, there were
many characters too among the women; life would never be
the same in that part of Belfast.

The mill with all its rigour, represented the realities of the
lifestyle of the neighbourhood but nearby they indulged in the
pleasures of their make believe world. Joe McKibbin's picture
house in Canning Street was a favourite rendezvous for the
locals. It was the only form of entertainment they could afford
and in some cases it was a place of rest and warmth for the
weary mill workers who sought escape from the crowded and
drab surroundings in which they lived. The price of admission
was 3d (three old pennies) and there was a daily matinee for
children at 1d admission. The story goes around that when

children could not get a penny Joe accepted jam jars instead of the usual penny. This story and others about Joe's have become a part of the folklore of the district and although it was destroyed in the blitz it lives on in the imagination of the younger generation who only know of the pre-war years and the terrible depression, from stories told by their parents or grandparents. There are few today who can imagine how difficult it was to afford the 3d that enabled those hard pressed workers to escape from the realities of life if only for a few hours.

The lifestyle of the community was closely linked with the neighbourhood churches and in every part of the city the air raids took a heavy toll of them. The north side of the city suffered very much in this respect and only a few remained out of a dozen or more. Throughout the city many old churches with their priceless windows and records were destroyed by bombs or fire. One of those destroyed was the Non-subscribing Presbyterian Church in York Street. It was a church associated with the local history but it had achieved widespread publicity on account of the eloquence of its minister Dr Arthur Agnew.

The doctor was a well-known speaker and his controversial pronouncements on a wide number of subjects, theological, humanitarian and political always attracted large congregations. But it was for his unstinted labours on behalf of the depressed people of the area that he will be best remembered. Dr Agnew guided and encouraged many young people to develop an interest in drama, art and literature. To advocate such ideas in the midst of the poverty and squalor that was part of the everyday life at the time was probably regarded by his friends as sheer madness. Nevertheless, in spite of the terrible conditions in which his people lived, many of them were encouraged by his help and friendly criticism of their early efforts. They continued with their studies and brought some fame to themselves and their city in the world of the arts, stage and literature.

The blitz destroyed his church but the Lion of York Street as he was known was not to be silenced. The church in York Street was not re-built but he was invited to share the pulpit at All Souls' Non-subscribing Church at Elmwood Avenue, where he remained until his death in 1977. From his ordination in 1923 Dr Agnew served God and his people for 54 years.

In York Street another well-known church was slightly damaged but not destroyed. This church, perhaps more than any other, associated itself with the poor and destitute of the dockland part of the city. The North Belfast Mission supervised by the Methodist community was better known as Daddy Maguire's. The church was so called by the locals as a mark of appreciation for the work of the minister during the time of great need in the city. The Rev. Maguire was indeed a father to all in need, Protestant, Catholic and non-believers. Perhaps the name went deeper than that. Perhaps it was something that only an Ulsterman could think up. The name Father is generally thought of as referring to a Catholic priest so the term Daddy was a compromise that offended no one. He opened a night shelter where young people, especially those who were turned out of their homes because their parents could no longer support them, could find a bed and a meal and perhaps help to enable them to get to England and find a job. There was an annex at the back of the church where he organised a breakfast room and soup kitchen. Mothers carried home pots of soup and bread from this kitchen to feed their children when they came home from school.

Daddy Maguire's trip to Bangor was a regular event and all the children of the area looked forward to it. For the most of the children, if not all, it was the only holiday they ever knew. Down the years the church retained the name given to it by the grateful people and the minister in charge was always Daddy Maguire to the locals. In the days after the raids the Mission helped with a great amount of welfare work and supplied meals to A.R.P. workers and demolition squads. In later years redevelopment scattered the congregation and the old church itself was demolished. Its passing marked the end of an era in the history of our city. The buildings mentioned in this section were not in D district but were in the adjoining area and came under the G district administration. This division, however, was for administration purposes only. The people of York Street, Tigers Bay, New Lodge Road and Carrick Hill were all the one community. They were the people of the mill and the docks.

In continuing the story of the lifestyle of the area something must be said about a famous bar and billiard hall. Readers may think that my choice of churches and a pub and billiard hall are a strange mixture, but the premises I have in mind were all accepted as part of the community and many boasted that they lived in close proximity to them.

Labourers, artisans, businessmen, lawyers and doctors all met on equal terms in the International. The International Bar stood at the corner of York Street and Donegall Street. It was an imposing building overlooking Royal Avenue, a main thoroughfare of the city. Few male members of the population at the time could say they had never been in the International Bar or billiard rooms. Many were drawn to it out of curiosity to see for themselves the world that lay inside the doors of that famed establishment.

The three upper floors were given over to billiards and no drinks were served in these rooms. Indeed many of the regular visitors were non-drinkers but enjoyed a game of billiards, especially in the pleasant atmosphere that was part of the International. The seating for the spectators was comfortable. Large wooden-backed benches stretched right around the beautifully decorated rooms with their ornate ceilings and panelled walls. Each room had eight tables and was heated by gas fires, an entirely different picture from that which one imagines at the sound of the name billiard hall. Among the visitors there were those who sat with their eyes fixed on the table following every stroke with an intensity as if they themselves were playing. Some never played because they could not acquire the knack of the game or could not afford the 6d or 1/- (a shilling) which was the price for the use of the table. The International was a place for good conversation and many of the world's economic and political problems were solved, at least in theory, within its confines.

The blitz not only destroyed a building, it took away part of the lifestyle, the atmosphere and the magic which bound together so many people who came from different walks of life. However, by some strange coincidence, the site of the International is still a centre for the local community. A small park now occupies the place where once it stood so proud, imposing and towering above the block of small shops that nestled beside it. In the summer, the seats and grass are occupied by locals and staff from the nearby offices and, no doubt, they still discuss the news headlines displayed outside the Telegraph offices not far away and give forth their views and offer solutions to the world's problems.

The pawnshop in pre-war days was part of the way of life in every working class district. The topic of the pawn gave the wits abundant opportunities to exercise their natural ability to change a tragic situation into a humorous one. I can well remember meeting a fellow one day who was walking along, unconcerned, with a suit tucked under his arm. He was obviously on his way to 'Uncle's', the word commonly used for the pawnshop. 'Have you no paper?' I asked, at the same time nodding towards the suit under his armpit. The question of his having to pawn the suit never arose, but I was genuinely surprised that he had made no attempt to parcel it up. People still retained a little pride and they usually wrapped their pledges in newspaper when brown paper was not available. The womenfolk in particular were sensitive about this and would hide their parcels under their shawls. Jackie knew I was surprised at his carrying the unwrapped suit and he replied, 'Jimmy, never be ashamed to go to the pawn. It's when you have nothing left to pawn that you will have to start to worry.'

I always remembered his reply. It was full of the realism of the time and I often asked myself, 'What was the position in a hungry household when there was nothing left to pawn?' In my own home we had a few regular pledges. There was always Father's suit or some of his tools and the head off Mother's sewing machine which I carried on the few occasions she had to pawn it, as it was rather heavy. Father did not like to pawn his tools and so his suit was used when necessary. If however, money was really needed, Father might go reluctantly to his tool box and select some pieces for which he thought he would get the money needed to pay the rent or some other pressing bill. He would wrap them up carefully and go out. I did not like to see him go to his tool box on these occasions because even as a boy I realised that it hurt him to have to pawn his tools. He was very much attached to them and handled them with care. I often watched him as he sat for hours honing his chisels and plane irons.

The pawnshops were well established as part of the social fabric and were scattered throughout the city. Every district had at least three or four of them. The blitz destroyed one particular pawnshop which down the years had gained some fame for itself, far beyond the boundaries of the locality in which it was situated. Adam Barr's pawn was in Great Patrick Street and many tales were told about Adam's as the locals fondly referred to it. The stories, handed down and repeated, became part of the folklore of the district. It was sufficient to say 'I'm away to Adam's' and your listeners knew exactly where you were going and why. Adam's was situated a few hundred yards from the Labour Exchange or the 'Bur-oo' as it was better known among the locals. Adam's pawn shop was established in Great Patrick Street many, many years before the idea of unemployment benefit came into existence. However, its position did help to widen the circle of publicity which it enjoyed. The employment exchange was the only one in the city. There were no area offices as there are today. Unemployed people in receipt of benefit or registering for work had to pass Adam's on the way to the 'Bur-oo' and, in the words of an old saying, they killed two birds with one stone. They brought their pledges with them as they went to sign on and redeemed them when they received their benefit later in the week.

An extra 6d or a shilling (2½ or 5 pence) could have always been bargained for at Adam's on a decent pledge and Adam knew when that extra 6d or shilling was needed and he did not hold out too long on the bargaining. The extra money could mean a lot to a needy family especially when it was needed to pay the rent. Stories were told of how housewives in desperation made up parcels of complete rubbish in the way of clothing and offered them as a pledge for a shilling in order to get some food for their family. Adam never turned these women away and they in turn would redeem their pledges at the first opportunity and pay 1d interest on the transaction although they knew they had pawned utter rubbish.

Adam had a large stock of tools which had been pawned with him over the years by unemployed tradesmen who could never get the money gathered together to redeem them. When the war came and work became available Adam let his customers have the tools they needed, on trust, until they settled into work and earned a few weeks' wages. Adam was kind-hearted but the workmen were honest and returned and paid their debts, and bought new tools to replace those they had pawned years previously. These and many other stories lived on long after Adam's was destroyed. Adam was an elderly man but powerfully built. No one knew or could guess his age but the old people of the neighbourhood said they remembered him as a young man when they went to the pawn with their mothers. Adam did not open again for business and another part of the tradition of old Belfast died. The war brought some prosperity to the city and, although unemployment was still widespread, real grinding poverty never returned. The memory of the pawnshop and the hard times it represented are now a part of history and the pawnshops themselves have become sales rooms.

Many secrets perished among the parcels that he had pushed into the pigeon hole cabinets that covered the walls and stretched from the floor to the ceiling and extended around another large room at the back of the shop in which there was also a massive safe. No one knew his secrets but it was rumoured that he held pledges from the nobility and the wealthy as well as the poor. It was known that some people who had made good in America or Australia came back to Belfast years later and asked Adam if it would be possible that a certain piece of jewellery or a watch could still be on the premises. On such occasions, the story is told, Adam would smile and say, 'Yes, it's about here somewhere. I had a feeling when you left it with me that if it were possible you would be back. I can always see how sad it is for people to part with certain things. They never seem to forget them and I never feel that I own them.'

Such was the philosophy of this giant of a man who became part of the folklore of the dockland community of Belfast. But then, of course, Adam understood the people.

14   *The post raid period*

For some months after the blitz, the city remained a ghost town, especially at night, but it slowly returned to some form of normality. The ugly burned-out remains of buildings which bore witness to the horrors of the raids were demolished and the sites cleared. People were returning to the city and the streets began to show signs of life and activity. The return was slow but steady and each day brought new life. When one considers that after the Easter blitz more than 100,000 left the city and thousands more followed them after the second big blitz in May, it is easy to imagine just how lonely and deserted Belfast really was. However, things were improving, and it was no longer the ghost town that we had experienced for months. It had been lonely and at times frightening to walk through the deserted streets which had been the scene of so much slaughter. On such patrols our only companions were an occasional screeching cat or snarling dog which at times made our hair stand on end. The unexpected sound of an animal in those dark and lonely streets was certainly frightening, especially when it resembled the screams of a child or woman in distress.

At this time I experienced a double sense of loneliness. When my duties were finished I had nowhere to go. My family was still away and as yet I was unable to get any accommodation for us in the area. Like many others whom I had helped, I was not keen to leave the district in spite of all the hardships encountered by remaining there. Each night I would sit about the post or patrol the streets until tiredness overtook me and I would then lie down on the floor with my haversack under my head and fall asleep. At last I found some accommodation in the form of a very badly damaged house but emergency

109

repairs were carried out to make it habitable and my family were able to come together again. In contrast to the conditions in which I had lived for the previous months, our new home was like a mansion to me.

At the post, enquiries about house repairs were our greatest problem. This was a matter entirely outside our control but the residents continued to bombard us with their complaints. All we could do in these circumstances was to suggest to the foremen on the sites that some individual family really needed immediate emergency repairs to be carried out.

To cope with the mammoth task of repairing upwards of 56,000 houses, an emergency squad of workers was recruited from all over the country including the South. There were hundreds of these workers and this created a new and some-what comical situation. The squads of workers were brought in to make the damaged houses habitable for homeless people, but they themselves wanted to be housed locally. Most of them came from rural areas and had never been to the city before. They did not know their way about and they thought it would be more convenient to live near their work.

To meet the demand for accommodation a new and enter-prising type of woman appeared on the scene. These were the landladies, some of whom were locals, but most came from the country and acquired large houses on the main roads and converted them into boarding houses for the migrant workers.

Emergency repairs were carried out on roofs, doors and windows. Plastering and other repairs were carried out later on. Thousands of windows had been broken and reglazing was out of the question. The immediate problem was solved by nailing roofing felt over the window frames. The next attempt to repair the windows was carried out using a linen-like material which was stretched and nailed over the window frames. This material was an improvement on the felt as it permitted the light to penetrate but the rain also soaked through it. Later, a real glazing operation was mounted by using what became known as war time glass. It let the light in but it was not transparent. People objected strongly to this glass especially when they were told it was not a temporary measure but that they would be stuck with it till after the war. It is difficult to imagine how depressing it was to sit in a room and gaze at a window without seeing what was going on outside.

The final operation came after the war when supplies of glass became more plentiful. Once more an army of glaziers descended on the city and for weeks the streets rang with the sound of tinkling glass as glaziers sat in the streets on little stools chipping window frames and re-glazing them with ordinary glass. 'That's rale glass now,' I heard an old lady say one day as I passed by one of those final glazing operations.

The migrant workers brought some new colour to the neighbourhood with their broad accents and a rare kind of wit. They created confusion in the shops when the shopkeepers could not understand them or when they used some strange sounding name for something they wished to buy. The important thing was that they came to do a job and they performed miracles. Those houses that we had looked at with despair in the early morning light just after the raids were now like the phoenix rising from the ashes.

During the emergency I served in a temporary position with the full time wardens and then I was offered a full time job. I accepted the offer but only after a lot of heart searching. There was a lot of restructuring and training necessary if civil defence was to be ready to meet future raids. The knowledge and equipment which took us through the blitz would have to be reappraised. I had the liking and ability to carry out this work, but the wages offered were ridiculously low. At this stage I feel I must refute any suggestion that civil defence workers were paid fabulous wages and were a burden on the rates and taxpayers. The wage paid for a 60 hour week based on a 12 hour day, from 7 in the morning to 7 at night, was £2.50 and, when I finished, my wages, which included three service increments, only amounted to £3.8.1 (about £3.40 pence). There were no special rates for night shifts. No overtime rates were paid and all time spent on call out and training was treated as voluntary. Those who spread those stories in most cases earned twice and three times as much for doing work that carried no responsibility. Thankfully, there were others who knew the facts and thought we were a crazy lot, but as we saw it, we had a very special job to do and we stayed with it in spite of the whispered innuendoes.

Belfast was among the heaviest bombed cities in the United Kingdom but it was fortunate that it did not experience the kind of horror weapons used on some cities in Great Britain. It was weapons such as oil, phosphorus, anti-personnel bombs and other powerful devices that we would have to prepare ourselves to meet with in the future. The oil bomb was a horrible weapon which consisted of a large bomb-like container filled with highly inflammable spirits and crude oil. The bomb exploded on impact scattering blazing oil which turned everything in its path including human beings into flaming torches. The phosphorus or flower pot bomb proved itself to be a ghastly weapon. The main feature of this bomb which gave it its name was a number of flower pot-shaped containers filled with phosphorus. These were packed into a large thin-cased container together with a variety of other incendiary agents and a number of explosive grenades. The whole package was detonated by a charge which split the case and scattered the deadly contents. It was certainly a nasty and dangerous box of tricks for any firefighter to come up against.

The anti-personnel bomb was a formidable weapon used mainly to cause the utmost disruption and casualties among civilians and civil defence workers. They were dropped in large numbers from containers and were fitted with delayed action fuses and anti-handling devices, which the Germans kept changing, thus making it more difficult for the bomb disposal crews to defuse them. Like incendiary bombs they were dropped during bombing raids and were a hazard to rescue teams and firefighters, many of whom were killed or injured as they climbed over debris or entered burning buildings. In rural areas they disrupted harvesting or killed livestock which triggered them off as they lay hidden in the grass or hung on bushes. Organised search parties went through the fields where these booby trap devices were reported to have been found. The drill for such a search followed a fixed pattern. The team stretched out and moved slowly across the field keeping away from bushes which were examined separately. If a suspicious object was located the finder would stop immediately and signal the rest of the team to do likewise. The position of each find would be indicated by a coloured ribbon and marked on a sketch map of the field. Dangerous fields were closed to the public and livestock until the bombs were removed or made safe. This is a sample of the type of weapons which civil defence workers had to contend with and more sophisticated horrors were introduced as the war developed. Belfast escaped these devices but the civil defence had to prepare for attack here in the future.

The big problem, however, was the fear of another incendiary raid. The incendiary blitz in May drove home the lesson of how inadequate our fire service was to control the great number of fires that could now be expected in any future raids and it must be understood that the government had no information that would suggest that the Germans would not be back again. The water supply for firefighting was something that had been entirely neglected. The firemen had no water supply other than the street hydrants and many of them had not been checked for years and in some cases they were not attached to the system.

Recruitment, equipment, a complete overhaul of existing training methods and the introduction of a system that would ensure an emergency water supply, were problems which had to be tackled as soon as possible.

On the training side, tactical deployment and reinforcing exercises drew attention to the fact that equipment was not standardised throughout the country. Local councils were responsible for maintaining the fire service and had failed to equip them on modern lines. The same problem arose in Great Britain where it was discovered that when firemen went to reinforce another city under attack it was usual to find that their stand pipes and hoses did not fit the fire hydrants in the areas where they were called to help. This problem arose for the Southern brigades when they came North during the blitz.

Fresh legislation was introduced and a new fire service known as the National Fire Service (N.F.S.) was organised throughout the United Kingdom. The new authority was empowered to purchase and standardise equipment. The auxiliary fire service was stood down. The reorganised service was manned by a freshly recruited full-time staff but there was still a lot of voluntary work in the areas outside the city.

The new service was responsible for ensuring that an adequate water supply for firefighting was available. A new section in the fire service was established and the fire authority was empowered to take control of ponds, mill dams and all available water supplies. Pipelines were laid from the docks to the centre of the city. The steel pipes capable of carrying a strong force of water were brought along High Street and Chichester Street. Massive water tanks were built in the city centre and in populated areas. There was an enormous tank, probably one of the largest in the British Isles, built on the big blitzed site in High Street. The tanks were filled with water and were maintained and kept clean by members of the new pipeline section. The service was supplied with new powerful pumps and other modern equipment. What a service we now had in comparison to the undermanned and ill equipped old Belfast fire brigade which stood against the savage attacks on our city. Other branches of the civil defence, the rescue and ambulance service were also improved and enlarged.

The wardens remained an independent group depending on their own initiative and relations with the local community. The improvements in the other services, however, did strengthen their morale by knowing that the back-up response to any call for help would be more readily available. The immediate problems of the wardens still came from the local residents and as more and more people returned to their homes the pressure on the wardens for information and other help increased.

Although we took an interest in the work being carried out in the district, our main task was to concentrate on building up and training our own small group. At this time a new section aimed at recruiting civilian firefighters was introduced and placed under the control of the wardens. The plan envisaged an operation in which local people would form street groups of firefighters. Recruitment and training of this new section became another part of the wardens' duty. I had seen this idea put into practice already during the blitz when men without any kind of training joined us in our efforts to control the fires which threatened to engulf their neighbourhood. At the post we were enthusiastic about the scheme and there was no doubt that we would be successful in building up a good body of street firefighters.

I was nominated to attend a course for instructors and, on

qualifying, I took charge of the organising and training of the new recruits. Corrugated iron huts were erected on waste ground and training was carried out at these sites. The huts, known as fire huts, were set up with some old furniture and damp straw. The place was splashed with a liberal quantity of paraffin oil to create a real heat effect and the damp straw produced plenty of smoke. Practice incendiary bombs were used to demonstrate how fires started and spread during incendiary attacks. The practice bombs burned and spluttered scattering pieces of flaming material which set fire to other objects in the hut. These conditions bore some resemblance to reality and we used them in teaching safety measures and protective procedures. Now that explosive incendiaries were being used, this situation was demonstrated by putting a thunderflash in the fire hut and recruits were shown how to fight the fire from behind cover until the thunderflash exploded or sufficient time elapsed to suggest that there were no explosive incendiaries in the hut. The introduction of the booby trap incendiary meant that firefighters had to take care and could not dash in to extinguish a fire in the early stages without some thought for their own safety. Live firefighters were better than dead or injured ones.

The training was divided into two parts. I put them through stirrup pump drills, taught them how to enter a room, how to move about in smoke and search a room quickly for casualties, and how to get them out. Most important of all was how to assess fire and the dangers of sudden spread. Never go into a burning building alone except to save life was my advice to all my recruits. Instruction and practice was thorough before the trainees fought real fires at the fire huts. The new recruits were always anxious to get a chance of tackling a real fire, but theory and practice were equally important. Although the fires were for practice purposes they were still real fires and any type of fire could be dangerous. From time to time I pointed out to them that they were not only preparing to fight fires during an air raid but that the skills they were learning could some day save a life or property if a fire broke out in their own home or that of a neighbour. This approach appealed to most of them when they saw a practical use for the training.

Then came the big night when the fires were set up at the fire hut. It was a community function. The whole neighbourhood turned out to watch. The wardens demonstrated stirrup pump drill and then proceeded to put out the first fire using all the safety procedures and at the same time I gave a commentary for the benefit of the public and especially for the firefighters before they went into action. The fires were re-kindled and the firefighters took over. This was the real test. Theory can do no more than teach caution and techniques.

The crackle of the flames, the blinding heat, the choking smoke and the sense of isolation all had to be contended with in a real fire. The training was good for the trainees. It brought out character and a sense of comradeship and helped them to handle fear. I met men some years after the war who told me in confidence that the training had taught them self-discipline.

Each firefighting team consisted of three members numbered 1, 2 and 3. Number 3 maintained the water supply and kept contact with Number 1 by calling out to him at intervals 'All right number 1?' who in turn would reply 'All right, number 3?' This procedure ensured that Number 1, the firefighter, was in no difficulties and that he was conscious at all times. Number 2 controlled the pump and kept up a steady flow of water. In a long operation all positions were interchangeable. It will readily be understood that no one would be expected to pump continuously or remain in a smoke-filled room over a prolonged period. Changeover was carried out by means of a drill designed to cause little or no disruption in the fire-fighting operation.

When the training programme was finished the recruits were supplied with a distinctive type helmet, respirators, overalls and armbands. Street parties had their own leaders who were responsible for equipment and prompting continued interest among their members.

Advanced training widened the contact with the National Fire Service. Training included practice with trailer pumps, emergency water supplies, hose and coupling drills. This training enabled the fireguards to work more effectively with the N.F.S. on the ground. The new co-operation may best be summed up by the following slogan:

The Fireguards prevent it Starting

The National Fire Service prevent it Spreading

The battle of the flames continued to be the main problem to confront the civil defence forces in all the theatres of the war. Firefighting tactics were continuously under review and a new organisation based on the old street team system and to be known as the fireguards was launched, in order to further the firefighting plans for the protection of the city. The fireguards became part of a nationwide organisation with better equipment and training facilities while retaining a community identity. They were organised at district level and in D district, Jim Davidson, an enthusiastic and efficient organiser, was appointed as district fireguard officer. I continued my interest on the instructional and tactical planning side of the new force and qualified as a tactical instructor.

Each new weapon introduced added a further threat to the civil population and civil defence planning was continuously under review. In spite of the marked advances in aerial warfare the warden maintained an important role in the defence of the home front. The development of saturation bombing and subsequent fire storms as experienced by the people of Hamburg and Tokyo led to new thinking on such things as damage control and assessment of fire situations. In early raids both here and in Great Britain, destruction of a single street or a large block of shops was considered to be a serious incident. New thinking and planning now faced the problem of whole neighbourhoods being severely damaged by saturation bombing raids carried out by a large number of aircraft.

The fire service had already been restructured and the problem of maintaining an adequate water supply independent of the normal hydrants was well in hand. There remained, however, the necessity for a new shelter programme and civil defence planning and a new look at damage control and the deployment and the most economic and efficient use of available services. Damage control came under radical change to meet the new developments.

During the blitz each post reported damage no matter how trivial to its district control centre. These reports, some of which were understandably exaggerated or hurriedly despatched, swamped the control centres and resulted in services, when available, being sent to minor incidents while major damage was neglected. A new system combining

damage assessment, reporting and control was introduced.

In operating this system, full responsibility for control on
the ground was given to one person who was to be known as
the incident officer and all reports of damage were to be sent to
him. His duty was to assess damage and the casualty situation
and to recognise any hazards to operations such as the spread
of fire and flooding. Such information was essential when it
came to making decisions on priorities or deploying services to
particular sites of damage in his area of control. With the new
system, all incoming services reported to the incident officer
and placed themselves under his overall control. It was up to
the incident officer to give a full, clear briefing to the officer in
charge of the incoming services to give him his priorities and to
discuss any known hazards including U.X.B.'s and the casualty situation. In the face of a changing situation he would
have to keep those in charge of the different services informed
of any new developments that would effect the operation.
Outgoing ambulances were instructed to tell the control point
the number of casualties being removed so that a check on the
likely number of casualties at the various sites could be kept
under constant observation and amended as each ambulance
left. The work of the incident officer or the I.O., as he was
known, carried great responsibility. He had to make quick
decisions based on reports coming into him from his wardens.
He had to possess tact in a great capacity to ensure the
co-operation of the officers in charge of the incoming services
who were used to making their own decisions and reporting to
their own depots or stations. Now they found themselves
co-operating with a stranger who had to impress them as to his
ability and the soundness of his decisions. Of course, the
secret of success, as I found it, was to direct the experts where
to work, never how to work, and to assist them in any way
without interfering.

The appointment of incident officers varied in different
regions. Some had a pool of incident officers who were sent by
controllers into heavily damaged areas. Other regions, including Northern Ireland, aimed at having trained officers
attached to the wardens' posts. In each case the I.O. depended
on his wardens who knew what needed to be done and in

many cases did the groundwork for the I.O. to take over. The nature of the operation often necessitated the setting up of an incident officer's post some distance from the facilities of the wardens' post. In such circumstances he had no telephone and in some cases his only light was supplied by hurricane lamps. This was before the days of computers, and all important information relating to casualty figures, fires, available services or withdrawals had to be drawn up on rough posters and kept up to date as each piece of information was added. Situation reports were compiled and sent to the wardens' post and control centre. All this information had to be logged, memorised and acted on by the I.O. and his team of wardens.

I was selected to attend a training course for incident officers. Instruction consisted of lectures on damage control procedures followed by tactical and realistic exercises in which our handling of the various situations was assessed. The final examination was very searching and covered such items as preparing situation reports, logging messages as they were received and the action to be taken. Also included was a briefing of incoming services based on information supplied. All this had to be done quickly and efficiently to avoid delaying the other services. The examination was designed to be tough and gave those who weathered it confidence in their ability to carry out the duties and procedures of their new office. The designation incident officer was regarded in civil defence circles as a high honour, but it was no more than a piece of paper if incident officers did not have a team of well trained wardens who knew what was expected of them and were willing to co-operate with him. The officer could not always be present at his post. At times it was best that he go and see for himself what was going on and to make his own assessments.

The functions of an incident officer were fully tested in all our future exercises including a few all night large ones. At these exercises the officers in charge of the other services and the police often showed surprise when they discovered that the officer in charge of operations was no more than a mere youth. I never experienced any reluctance on the part of the other officers to co-operate with me and I think we gained a lot by working together and exchanging ideas.

The neglect in providing a proper shelter programme prior
to the blitz must go down as one of the greatest mistakes made
by the authorities in their handling of the defence of the city.
The idea that the enemy could never get this far and financial
wrangling as to where the responsibility for supplying shelters
lay, led to the great disaster in terms of civilians killed and
seriously injured. The Anderson shelters which proved
effective in Great Britain were not introduced into Northern
Ireland. Deep shelters were not practical owing to the nature
of the clay on which Belfast was built. The shelters provided
were not in sufficient numbers and were badly designed and
constructed. The most distressing disasters occurred in some
of the overcrowded shelters. People flocked into the only
shelters available and, unfortunately, when they were hit
there was a terrible carnage owing to the large numbers
involved. The loss of life and injuries both in the shelters and
the unprotected streets forced the authorities to reassess their
shelter policy.

A new type of shelter known as the Morrison shelter was
distributed to households where suitable space for its erection
was available. The shelter was a strong table-like steel construction and was delivered in a kit form which was assembled
in the house. It could be fitted with a mattress and other
amenities and made ready for use in an emergency. The
Morrison shelter proved itself unpopular owing to its bulk and
ugly appearance. While some people tried to brighten them a
little by decorating the sides with coloured curtains or displays
of flower arrangements or a collection of ornaments on top,
others dismantled them and left them in their backyards or
gardens to rust.

A new shelter which was designed to move with the blast of
a bomb was approved and work was started on building them
throughout the city. The principle was simple. The shelter was
built on a concrete base which was laid on top of a sheet of
roofing felt and was not attached or sunk into the road surface.
The shelter was reinforced with steel rods which tied it
together in a solid mass. I saw pictures where shelters had
swung right round as if they had been on a pivot, and others
showed relatively undamaged shelters that had been pushed
two or three feet from their original position. The pictures

were even more impressive when compared with the scenes of total destruction all around them.

The wardens became involved in the shelter programme and it was their duty to recruit and organise a new section in civil defence to be known as the shelter marshals. Shelters were fitted with doors and the aim of the new section was to recruit local residents who would be willing to keep the keys and open the shelters on an alert. The idea caught on and there was no trouble in recruiting suitable people who welcomed the opportunity to offer their services. The marshals, both women and men, carried out their duties with enthusiasm and kept the shelters clean and ventilated. Small amenities such as water containers, first aid boxes and in some cases emergency lighting were installed by the more capable and experienced marshals. Later, with the help of the wardens, they drew up a roll of the residents who would be expected to be in the shelter in the event of an emergency. This information was added to the wardens' record cards which had proved so useful at the time of the blitz.

As I write about this phase of the warden's work I can now see it as an early step in community care and involvement so much discussed today. The new look shelters and the presence of the marshals relieved the wardens of the anxiety they experienced while trying to persuade the people to take shelter and the vivid memories that haunted us of those who had suffered by not taking our advice.

In future the shelters would be clean, cheerful, comfortable and safer. This was a sharp contrast to the dark dungeons where many had taken shelter from the terror of the night.

Life in the civil defence was not all confined to training, otherwise it would have been a dull affair. The social side had its place, and dances, social evenings, parties, concerts and get-togethers were a regular part of the activities among the volunteers. There was a vast amount of theatrical talent among the members and the highlight of the entertainment was the annual concert which consisted entirely of contributions by C.D. personnel. The concerts were a great success and engaged the talents of many other members who made costumes and scenery for the event.

Craft groups were organised at post and district levels and a course in basic woodwork and the use of tools was organised at the College of Technology for civil defence volunteers. The friendly rivalry generated added to the popularity of the scheme. Local exhibitions were held and the whole effort culminated in an exhibition of selected articles which were hung in the Belfast Art Gallery, now the Ulster Museum. I was successful on two occasions in having my work exhibited at the museum. It was an honour which was equally shared by my companions at the post.

All these activities, including darts matches and quizzes, helped to maintain interest and fill the time during the long, dreary war years. The quiz was a popular form of entertainment and created a healthy rivalry between posts and districts. When the competitions became inter-district, the big guns came out. Post 381 was always well represented on the district team and excitement and enthusiasm grew as the competition reached the finals. D district was always very successful in these competitions and I remember one of the wits at the post saying 'Don't worry, lads, if you can't beat them you will scare them.'

As well as being entertaining, the quiz was a painless form of training and the ministry decided to offer a trophy and the competition was now extended across the whole province. It was known as the Hayes Cup and every post competed for the honour of representing their region or district. The test covered all aspects of a warden's duties. There were tests in first aid, emergency rescue and firefighting, at various centres. The tests then became more personal. The judges visited the posts and inspected records and filing methods as well as equipment and the way it was stored and maintained. Then came the most gruelling part of the test. Each member of the team was interviewed by a panel of judges who shot questions at them, not only on matters relating to civil defence but also about their personal interests, hobbies, sport and general topics. At the end of this round, Post 381 was chosen to represent D District in the final of the competition. The process of elimination started all over again but this time the going was stiffer. The competition was now set to select the champions from among the champions.

The final inspection and interviews were as frightening as

the blitz itself. On our previous record the district officers and companions at the post expected us to win. So high was the confidence of all around us that the very thought of failure made us more nervous. We just had to win. Each man felt that he was responsible for the success of his team, as indeed he was because at this stage it was practically an individual test.

The judges were all ex-army officers who had attained the rank of captain or major. The standard expected by these experienced officers was high and as we were strangers to them, we had to sell ourselves to them in one interview. The night finished with refreshments and general conversation but the judges did not give any information or hint in any way as to how we had impressed them. We waited anxiously as the competition continued in the other areas and we were sure that our competitors had the same anxious moments.

At last the long awaited news came from headquarters. Post 381 were the winners of the coveted trophy. The trophy was presented by the minister for public security at a packed concert in the Ulster Hall. It was a great achievement and we felt proud as we stood in front of a vast applauding audience. We felt proud not only for ourselves but for the honour of our post and the volunteers who had worked so hard in action and in lull time. We were sure they shared our pride as they sat in the audience and clapped and cheered our victory.

I was to receive many more congratulations in the years to come but the excitement and tension connected with the winning of the Hayes Cup ranks high among my memories. In spite of my age and youthful appearance more responsibility was offered to me and at 23 I became the youngest group warden in the entire service.

Civil defence personnel often took part in ceremonies and parades organised by armed services. As civil defence personnel did not practice ceremonial drills we were generally brought together and given some instruction on drill and words of command. Considering that we did not have any regular practice and that there were always new faces at each turnout we always did credit to the service. It was amazing how we kept in line and in step. One such parade, which today might be received with some concern and perhaps hostility, was organised as a salute to the Red Army. A Russian general took the salute at the City Hall which was bedecked with Russian flags and emblems. Donegall Place and the surrounding buildings were also gaily decorated with Russian flags and pennants. Even the Americans did not receive such a colourful expression of solidarity as the Russians received that day in the streets of Belfast. I had taken part in several parades but this was certainly the largest one of its kind. So far as I can recall I never saw so many servicemen marching in the city. There was also a large contingent of R.U.C. members, all big men and of equal size, marching together and this in itself was a splendid sight. The firemen, civil defence and nursing services all marched like veterans. The Russian general must have been impressed at that colourful parade as he stood and took the salute.

My next parade was unexpected and unrehearsed but it also turned out to be a memorable occasion. One evening I received a message that I was to report to the Pollock Dock the next day. Full dress was to be worn and I was to be there no later than 2 p.m. That was the full text of the message. No other details were given but I guessed I was to take part in some kind of welcoming ceremony. As I have said civil defence personnel were usually given a little prior warning about such functions in order to give them some briefing or to practise their drills. This time, however, there was no warning and I could only conclude that we were going to meet some V.I.P. and for security reasons no prior notice was given.

There were representatives from all the armed forces, the police, fire service, nursing staff from the local hospitals and the different sections of the civil defence. The army and marine band in full dress uniforms lent a splash of colour to a glorious summer day. We soon became overheated and parched as we stood in the open square with the blazing sun beating down on us.

As we waited a whisper went through the ranks. The expected visitors were the King and Queen. The excitement banished our tiredness and we held ourselves erect. There was a roll of drums as the bandsmen struck up the anthem and we stretched ourselves to our full height as we stood to attention.

The gathering was not large and the atmosphere was homely and friendly. There was no sign of strain on their

Majesties as they strolled about amongst us. The Queen chatted at some length with the ladies. His Majesty did not speak but lingered with each person and smiled or nodded in a friendly way as he passed among us. It was a unique occasion with a spirit all its own that differed from the pomp and ceremony normally attached to royal visits. There were no flags or decorations in the square. Neither were there any crowds or police other than those taking part in the ceremony. This was the visit of their Majesties to thank those who were serving the nation.

The International Bar, 1939.   (Bailey Collection)
This building was very much part of the pre-war way of life. (See page 105). *The blitz
reduced it to a pile of rubble.*

15   A walk down memory lane

The war years were grim and dreary but in spite of this there are few who remember those years who have not some happy memories of people they met, of funny and unexpected happenings and lasting friendships even if they only continued by the exchange of letters. It was the little pleasures that stirred us most and left lingering memories that still come back at unexpected moments. Let me take you then down that lane of memories to those far-off days when we sang 'When the lights go on again all over the world'.

The most memorable event apart from the blitz was the arrival of the Yanks. The first landing of the American forces in Europe took place in Northern Ireland on the 24th January 1942. 'Things will never be the same again,' I heard an old fellow say. 'Yes, mark my words,' he continued, 'I remember those boys in France during the last war. I tell you, things will never be the same.'

He was right, things never were the same again, such was the impact the American boys made on the lifestyle of the Ulster people, especially in the rural areas. Belfast and Londonderry, the two cities of Northern Ireland, also came under the influence of the American way of life. The presence of the Americans was felt in the dance halls, bars, restaurants and hotels. Even card players changed from the usual game of pontoon (21) or solo to the Yankee game of poker. The open air schools of pitch and toss, or two up as the Australians call it, gave way to playing dice, due no doubt to American influence.

The Yanks did not have their own way all the time, and there are stories still told of how the local lads put one over on them. Whiskey was scarce and the Yanks were able to pay well above the market price for it. They did not always get whiskey for their money and those who bought poteen were lucky. In many cases they bought weak black tea with a little whiskey in it in order to give it the right smell.

Whirlwind romances were part of the pattern that marked the passage of the Yanks throughout the various theatres of war. Many young Ulster girls married their Johnny Dough-boys and forged another but more modern link between America and Ireland. The Ulster brides were not the only ones: the Yanks found their future wives in all parts of the world. Their romantic exploits brought a new word into use. 'G.I. Brides' was a term used in relation to the marriage of American servicemen to local girls.

The Americans' demand for transport in the city produced many innovations in an attempt to meet the demand. Taxis and cars could not operate owing to strict petrol rationing but the local boys showed their ingenuity. They too believed in earning a quick dollar. Horse-drawn carriages soon appeared on the streets. There were dozens of them and they sprang up so quickly it seemed as if we had been carried back in time to the stage-coach days. The horse-drawn carriages did indeed resemble the old stage-coaches but in fact they were old funeral carriages which had been brought out of retirement. In the city centre, especially at night, the sound of the motor cars and hooting of horns was replaced by the clip-clop of horses hooves and the tinkling of small bells and horse brasses as the carriages with their passengers glided past in the darkness.

There was another enterprising, well known colourful character who took the engine and back end away from a beautiful Daimler and had it adapted so that it could be drawn by a horse. The horse-drawn limousine became a well known spectacle in the city centre not only on account of the car. The driver himself was a man of unique qualities and he exhibited a flair for real showmanship as he drove through the city perched on top of the bonnet wearing a large stetson hat, a leather jacket and a crimson red spotted scarf around his neck. The Yanks sat back in comfort enjoying every moment of the fantastic ride and their amazing cabby.

Volumes could be written on the exploits of the Yanks and the characters who set about to supply their needs. There are still many families in different parts of the province whose daughters fell in love and married some of those young men who walked our streets and roads so many years ago.

It must be a bit of a mystery to young people to listen to stories about food rationing when they see the ever growing number of supermarkets with their vast stocks. The older citizens will have many memories as they recall their own experiences of wartime shortages. Rationing was introduced to ensure fair shares in a situation where even the basic necessities were in short supply.

In Northern Ireland, tea, sugar, butter, eggs and meat were rationed but we were a little better off than the mainland where bread, milk and potatoes were also rationed. The judicious use of rations was an essential science that the housewife had to master. Many had already gained ample experience of making do during the pre-war depression when they had to make ends meet to ward off hunger and malnutrition. When the war came there were queues for everything. A woman could well have stood in a queue for hours while doing her shopping. But they got used to it and in a way the queues became a meeting place for exchanging ideas and airing complaints. But often their patience was rewarded when the opportunity arose to purchase some little off-the-ration titbit that was on offer in the store.

Irishmen in general are noted for their reluctance to go shopping but during the war they surrendered to the temptation of picking up something extra or a few razor blades, and took their place in a queue. To the women who were used to queuing this appeared as something little short of a miracle because a lot of men at the time even left the purchase of their clothes to their wives or mothers. I remember standing in a queue one day feeling rather embarrassed. I queued for about 15 minutes and was subjected to some friendly banter, most of which I am sure could never be printed. However as I hurried home with my small treasures, namely a pot of marmalade and a bag of broken biscuits, I thought it was worth all the hassle.

There was one incident concerning rationing which I can recall vividly. My wife went away to stop with her sister-in-law who was about to have a baby and she had arranged to stay with her for a few weeks. I was not practised in the art of stretching the rations, especially the tea, and I ran out of it.

The shop where we registered was an old established family grocery-cum-druggist. The owner was an elderly, severe looking, strict but nevertheless kindly gentleman. His style of dress resembled that of a character direct from the pages of a Dickens' novel. Somehow the idea came to me to ask him for a quarter pound of tea in advance of the next ration period. He looked at me with his severe, disapproving manner and I felt like a schoolboy who had been sent before the headmaster to answer for some mischievous behaviour. 'Mr Doherty, borrowing tea from your next ration is not going to solve your problem,' he said. 'In fact it will put me in trouble when Mrs Doherty comes in next week for her groceries.' I was sorry I had thought of asking him: I felt trapped but I resisted the sudden impulse to run from the shop.

'Wait a minute and I will see what I can do,' he said, as he moved towards the staircase which led to his living quarters. He returned shortly with a packet of tea and said it was his own and that I could have it as a present. I thanked him profusely and made a hasty retreat from the shop.

As Northern Ireland was an agricultural area, basic foods were easy to come by. There was little black market trading, except in tea which was the most difficult thing to get. Even in the South where most things were available, the tea ration per person was lower than our own. The ordeal I went through for that packet of tea is one thing I have never forgotten and my wife and I still joke about it. When the conversation drifts to the days of rationing my wife will often say 'I think our grocer frightened Jim more than the bombs'. She is probably right.

Matches were in short supply; in fact they were almost impossible to get. How it was possible to get along without them was a miracle of the time. However, in wartime there was an answer to everything and the answer to the scarcity of matches was to produce home-made lighters. The lighters were made clandestinely in the engineering departments of the shipyards, aircraft factories and other engineering works. Some of them were well finished and could have competed in an open market with well-known models. Others were merely crude pieces of metal but they supplied a spark or a flame which was all that was needed. The wits had a field day when it came to the scarcity of matches and cigarette lighters.

One such story I rather liked recounted the visit of an official of the Air Ministry to the aircraft factory, during which he became engaged in conversation with one of the workers. 'How many have you worked on?' asked the official. 'Oh a hundred or more,' replied the fitter. 'Wonderful! Wonderful! Fighters or bombers?' pressed the visitor excitedly. The workman hesitated for a second or two and said 'Ach sure, sir, you've got it all wrong. I thought we were talking about lighters.'

Rationing brought a new kind of food and a new word into the larders and vocabulary of the Ulster housewife. Spam and dried eggs came from America and although they never took on here they were welcomed by the hard pressed British housewives. Spam was a form of processed meat intended for general use as part of the meat ration but in Northern Ireland it was only used as a filler for sandwiches. Dried eggs were received with derision and doubt when they were first offered as a substitute for real eggs. Each packet was the equivalent to 1 dozen eggs or a month's supply. The Ministry of Food issued recipes suggesting ways of preparing attractive and tasty dishes in order to interest housewives in the use of the dried eggs. One could get used to them and with a little experimentation a tasty meal could be set up, although they were a long way from the traditional 'Ulster Fry' of bacon and eggs and all the trimmings.

Like all war time innovations dried eggs caught the imagination of the humorists. One day I was in a school teaching gas mask drill when a little fellow said to me 'Mister, what did the hen say when she saw a packet of dried eggs?' I thought for a few seconds and said, 'I'm stumped, what did the hen say?' 'There go my crazy mixed up chicks,' was his quick reply. I thought the joke was very good and the little fellow enjoyed catching me out. The strain of the war years had not dampened spirits rather it tended to increase the ability to invent and spread stories and jokes.

Some common fruits and vegetables became a rarity and bananas disappeared completely. Children grew up during the war years with no knowledge of this delicious fruit other than perhaps a picture in a school book for teaching the alphabet, A for Apple, B for Banana. More important to the housewife was the scarcity of onions which made it difficult to prepare a tasty meal.

Food shortages and rationing were things that the nation was expected to endure. But we often complained, not fully realising how difficult it was to maintain the flow of food necessary to feed the nation. The men of the merchant navy knew what every case of tea or bag of sugar cost in human suffering. This loss of life was well known in our community. Part of our area was known locally as Sailortown. The sea was a tradition among these people and many families mourned a father, a son or both, who were lost at sea when German submarines attacked the food convoys on the Atlantic run. This terrible toll among our merchant fleet prompted the Ministry of Food to produce posters encouraging housewives and others to conserve food. Wartime recipes aimed at using every scrap of food and suggested alternative ingredients when the usual ones could not be obtained. I can recall one of these recipes which gave directions on how to make a table jelly using gelatine and fruit juice essence. I experimented on several occasions but wartime jelly was not a success. I abandoned my experiments and lived with the memories of my favourite flavoured jellies until they returned to our tables.

One important memory that should not be forgotten was the battle to sustain our linen industry during the war years because of its importance to the war effort. The industry depended on the supply of flax from Russia but the war cut off this source of raw materials and the spinning mills faced cutbacks and the threat of closure. Locally grown flax had been sufficient to maintain the industry in its early stages of development. Due, however, to the enormous demand for Irish linen, other sources for the supply of flax had to be found and Russia became the most important supplier.

Now, a vigorous drive to encourage the production of home grown flax was promoted and special legislation enabled the Ministry of Agriculture to take over large sections of uncultivated and neglected land in rural areas for the growing of flax. Farmers who had land available were encouraged to grow flax and were guaranteed a ready market and good prices. Flax became a topic of conversation not only in the country regions but also in the city. Planting the flax was a simple matter when compared with the problem of winning it when the harvest came. Harvesting the flax was always a difficult task in normal times but this massive undertaking needed an army of workers to make sure the crop would be saved. Hundreds of volunteers came forward to join this army, from the villages, the towns and the city. The entire population helped in some way to ensure the continuation of our linen production.

Voluntary groups of bank clerks, civil servants, shop assistants, unemployed workers, firemen and civil defence personnel left the city early each morning in lorries and fire service personnel carriers, bound for the countryside to do battle with the flax. For normal sized fields professional pullers were organised in groups and they went from farm to farm to pull the flax. In the large stretches commandeered by government order, the flax was cut by machinery. The volunteers, mostly white collar workers, found the going hard on these flax gathering expeditions. The work was backbreaking for the inexperienced. Trained farm hands showed the volunteers how to gather the flax quickly, tie it in sheaves and stooks, ready to be collected. Working in the open air improved the appetite and although the food was simple, a mug of tea, a few roughly cut slices of bread with jam or butter and an apple, it was warmly received when breaktime came. The food was usually brought on the tailboard of a trailer from the farm house and served in the field. On the large, open stretches of land where the numbers engaged were larger, the food was served from the back of one of the trucks and the workers came up and received a pre-packed lunch and a mug of tea from a large urn.

The linen industry survived the shortages of the war years and saved the jobs of those who knew no other kind of work except that connected with the mills. The battle to save the linen industry was of great importance to the province but it could not have succeeded without the co-operation and determination of the people.

Wartime radio ranks highly in the memories of the public. Apart from the songs certain programmes are still remembered as the greats of their time. I.T.M.A., It's That Man Again, shot to the top of the bill and held that position throughout the war years. Another well loved entertainer was

Vera Lynn, the forces sweetheart, and Northern Ireland had its own forces sweetheart, Bernie McCann. The Nine O'Clock News will always be remembered. This was the highlight of the day and people made a point of listening to it. Its call signal became a national symbol and a ray of hope for the captive people of Europe who risked their lives just to hear those few words of freedom 'This is the B.B.C. Home Service and this is the Nine O'Clock News'.

It was not only the B.B.C. which left us with our memories of wartime broadcasting. 'Germany calling, Germany calling' was the call signal of the traitor William Joyce, who broadcast German propaganda to the British people. It was hateful and hurtful especially when the United Kingdom stood alone and her ships and cities were being attacked. His voice had a leering, mocking sound which those who heard it will never forget. Most people learned to regard his broadcasts as a big joke. There were some who, on principle, would not listen to or discuss these broadcasts and there were others who went into fits of rage at the very sound of his voice. There were also those who shouted back at him, not always using the best of language. One night at the post we were listening to one of his usual tirades as he gloated on the success of the German submarines against our shipping. There was a fellow who was more disturbed than usual and shouted some remarks at the speaker. We always took his reaction to Lord Haw Haw's broadcasts as a piece of fun and some of the boys encouraged him to answer back. However, this particular night, with the exception of a few remarks, he just walked up and down clenching and un-clenching his fists. Then suddenly he shouted 'I'll shut that b . . . . . d up' and at the same time he lunged forward and sent the wireless flying across the room. We did not see him for a few days and then he returned and offered to pay for the damage to the wireless. Fortunately, however, the damage was not serious. We only needed two valves and a knob which we were able to get from a junk shop in Smithfield for a few shillings. New parts for wireless sets were impossible to get but this junk man dismantled old sets. He had hundreds of parts and old valves. His shop was a favourite haunt for amateur wireless enthusiasts and was known as the Ham Shop.

Danny was full of apologies 'I don't like that Lundy,' he explained in his own quaint way, 'but the other night he really got my goat.' Danny came from somewhere up the country and at times it would have taken an interpreter to translate some of his strange sayings. A good part of his vocabulary consisted of old Ulsterisms and although we pulled his leg from time to time, we all liked him and we were pleased to see him back. He was a seafaring man for the most of his life and it was Lord Haw Haw's bombastic broadcast about the German submarine attacks on our shipping that had upset him. Danny had retired from the sea some years before the war but his thoughts and feelings were still with the men of the merchant navy who braved the sea and the submarines, and brought in the food and other essentials so vital to us.

The people nicknamed William Joyce Lord Haw Haw on account of the exaggerated English upper class accent that he adopted in his broadcasts. Haw Haw had a habit of giving little pieces of local information no doubt with the intention of creating the impression that Germany had information available on what was going on in Great Britain. Most of these references were of a general nature and could have applied to a great number of places. As an example, one of his favourite pieces was to announce that the clock in a certain town square was slow or had stopped. Of course many of these old clocks had stopped or had been running slow for years, but in small communities such broadcasts caused suspicion among neighbours. Another source of local information was old holiday snapshots which German Intelligence collected and compared with up-to-date aerial photographs of the same areas. Haw Haw would use the information obtained from these photographs in his provocative broadcasts. 'We know that armament factories have been built' (naming the area) but I give you this warning. Our gallant airmen will raze them to the ground.'

This form of propaganda was dangerous and upsetting when rumours of third column activity were uppermost in people's minds. The full propaganda effects were magnified by those who listened to and digested every word that came from the villain's lips. People were apt to exaggerate when they discussed these broadcasts and brief ambiguous refer-

ences were enlarged and put in contexts that identified particular places. Two ships sunk soon became the loss of a full
convoy. The government, while advising people not to listen,
made no attempt to make listening a criminal offence.

The war years rolled on. Every day brought something new.
The press too had its good and bad days with the gloomy
headlines hidden and those which blazed across the front
pages and raised the hopes of the nation.

In June 1941 clothes rationing was introduced. Churchill
objected strongly to it when it was first suggested. 'Have the
people not suffered enough? At least leave them with their
dignity.' But the necessity for such a measure overruled all
arguments and clothes rationing became part of the history of
the home front. During the debates it was argued that as well
as saving material, about half a million workers engaged on
production and distribution would be released to serve in the
forces or to do essential war work. The housewife was faced
with the new worry of how best to use the clothing coupons.
Each article of clothing had its own fixed coupon value.
Rationing was strict and heavy penalties were imposed on any
shopkeeper found to be violating the regulations. Make do
and mend became a popular pastime with classes in dressmak-
ing springing up everywhere.

For a while clothes rationing did affect the cheerful accept-
ance of war time restrictions as Churchill had predicted. It hit
young men and women especially but it also caused concern
among the older members of the population, who in spite of
other discomforts still liked to dress well and keep in fashion.
The war brought some prosperity and even poorer people,
who out of necessity had always been obliged to use hand-me-
downs from other members of the family, now for the first
time in their lives experienced the pleasures of mass produced
fashionable clothes at reasonable prices. Their displeasure was
therefore all the greater when they found this new luxury
being snatched from them.

Rationing was not the only clampdown on the clothing
industry. Lavish design was also curtailed and clothing
became austere and drab. From the men's point of view the
restriction on the use of turn-ups at the bottom of trousers was
something that they found hard to accept. This has been an

accepted fashion in men's clothing in recent times but when it was introduced to save time and material men felt they were improperly dressed when they appeared without turn-ups on the bottom of their trousers. They overcame this restriction by a simple ruse. When buying or ordering a made-to-measure suit, they made sure the leg measurements were a few inches longer, than was necessary and they then proceeded to have turn-ups made from the extra material thus gained. Men did not consider this ploy as illegal or in any way discreditable. It was little dodges such as this that lent some colour and excitement to the drab existence of the war years.

Children missed out on a very important part of childhood during the war. They grew up without experiencing the sheer delight of unwrapping a new toy or bright eyed doll at Christmas. On looking back on our own childhood, we could recall the joy of Christmas toys. Now, even the modest tin clockwork motor car, which could have been purchased for a shilling or two and brought untold pleasure to the poorest families, could no longer be bought. Gone too were the cap-guns which gave days of endless fun to the children as they played cowboys and indians and re-enacted scenes from the silver screen.

Children during the war years were deprived of these luxuries. In their place, fathers and uncles made wooden trucks or locomotives, or cut animal shapes out of plywood and mounted them on wheels. Forts made of wood, and painted or camouflaged, were popular with the older boys especially if they could get a few lead soldiers. The girls did not fare so well. They had to be content with an old doll's face remade with a new rag body or a new set of clothes for a large doll made from one of their own old dresses. Where fathers were sufficiently skilled, they made their daughters a doll's house complete with miniature furniture.

Some of these hand-made toys are still preserved in many households by people who are themselves parents or even grandparents. They are treasured in memory of loving parents who tried so hard to bring the spirit of Christmas, as they themselves had known it, to their children. The old teddy bear that is so often thrown about from corner to corner but never discarded, is perhaps a relic of those wartime days.

Travel was difficult. Petrol rationing was strict and motoring for pleasure was not permitted. The use of beaches was restricted and many of them were mined. Local councils organized amusements in the parks. 'Holidays at home' became a new slogan. There were open air concerts, bands, sporting competitions for children, all the fun of the beach including tons of sand transported to the parks. The children made sand castles and there were the usual prizes for the best models. Parents, instead of taking their children to the nearby parks which the children knew well, often brought them to parks on the other side of the town thus creating a sense that they were indeed on holiday.

The dim outlines of some wartime slogans remained on walls for years after 1945 and brought back memories, thankfully, in most cases, happy ones. Hundreds of witty slogans appeared from time to time but there was one that caught the imagination and lived on even after the war. The source still remains a mystery. The magic word written in bold letters S.K.I.B.O.O. appeared on gable walls and roadways. According to the legend, Skiboo owned everything, knew everything and could do anything. It appeared on tanks in the desert war, Ulstermen serving in the desert brought a piece of Ulster across the world. Skiboo has all the hallmarks of originating in the Belfast shipyard which is famous for Ulsterisms as well as ships.

16   1944, the year of decision

1944 was the year of decision, the final act in the long drawn out drama of a war in which millions had died. Everywhere in occupied Europe there was new evidence of hope. The whole concept of the war was changing. In the race for final victory the power to destroy was all that mattered.

The Allies stepped up their air offensives. Heavy raids involving thousands of bombers and more devastating than anything the world had ever witnessed were launched against Germany and large industrial areas in occupied Europe. Talk of a second front was on everyone's lips. The end was in sight, but nothing short of complete defeat would induce the German armed forces to surrender. Hitler, in his broadcasts, kept the spirit of resistance strong by his boasts of new and terrible weapons which would soon be used against their enemies.

The closing phase of the war was now developing into a race in the scientific and technological field with each side hoping to produce weapons that would bring ultimate and quick victory. New weapons were in the process of production. Old devices were improved and science was being called upon more and more. Radar and anti-radar was being developed. New designs in aircraft, fitted with the most sophisticated bomb-aimers and capable of great speed and manouverability, were now in use. Bigger bombs packed with more powerful explosive substances and ingenious incendiary devices aimed at causing the greatest destruction and disruption of the German economy were part of the Allied offensive. The German home front had to be demoralised.

In view of this advanced technology, which of course was also being pursued by the Germans, it was felt that our civil defence training was trailing far behind, and it was essential that it should be brought up to date. A completely new approach to training was introduced for full time wardens. My involvement in this training course became one of the most interesting and amusing experiences in my work with civil defence. The course was arranged in two parts. The opening classes consisted of films showing pictures of actual damage, slides, lectures and discussions, and were conducted in the Assembly's College in what would certainly be considered an atmosphere conducive to study. The course was followed by a written examination for which graded certificates were presented to successful candidates.

At the same time a new publicity and recruiting drive was launched. New style posters appeared on walls and advertising space was acquired in local newspapers. The whole publicity exercise was not aimed solely at bringing in recruits. In addition, it was designed to alert the public and make them realise that civil defence could still have a role to play before the conflict was over.

In the examination I received a first class certificate and an invitation from the chief instructor to take charge of the demonstration team to be used in the second part of the course, which was conducted by Mr C. Larmour, assistant chief instructor. The venue for this part of the course was at Park Lodge on the slopes of Cavehill as they sweep down on to the Antrim Road near Bellevue. Park Lodge was at one time the residence of the Baird family, owners of the *Belfast Telegraph*, and was now the training college for the Northern Ireland Civil Defence Corps. The classes were smaller than those at the Assembly's College where we all met together in large lecture rooms. About 24 wardens took part in the course each week and it was spread out over a six weeks period and during that time the entire strength of the full-time wardens service passed through the school. The course was entirely practical, with few lectures except for a few brief instructions on procedures, and it was our intention to make the course beneficial, interesting and as enjoyable as possible for the wardens.

During this period we turned this old setting at the foot of the Cavehill into a world of fantasy. The demonstration team became actors and producers. Each week we set up new situations in order to get the incoming classes thinking for themselves and not to depend on what they had heard from their companions who had attended courses during the previous weeks. The object of the course was to demonstrate the dangers with which civil defence workers would have to contend and the action best suited for their own personal protection.

The course was part of a serious training programme but, of course, comedy and outright crazy situations crept in from time to time. I can recall one hilarious situation involving Pat McAllister, the heavy-weight boxing champion, long since retired at that time. He was a mountain of a man with an interesting repertoire of stories about his days in the ring and in the travelling circus. I am sure that later Pat added the tale of his adventure during gas training at Park Lodge to his repertoire. One day a gas warning was given unexpectedly and the students struggled into their gas masks as a cloud of gas drifted towards them. I say struggled because it was obvious that gas mask drill had been neglected for some time. Pat, however, was the most unfortunate. He had picked up someone else's respirator and had carried it with him believing it was his own. Pat tried to get the respirator, which was about three sizes too small for him, over his massive face. With the gas choking him and the straps of the gas mask catching his ears and chin, because that was as far as they could go, poor Pat certainly made a comical sight. I saw his difficulties and took him out of the gas into fresh air where he soon recovered. 'If the Danish Champion saw you now, Pat, he would think you were an easy taking,' I said jokingly. Pat never failed to give a round by round account of how he defeated the Danish Champion and he often produced an old battered pair of boxing gloves. He would hold them out for his listeners to see and smooth them fondly with a gentle stroke of his massive hand and say, 'There they are, these are the gloves I wore the night I defeated the Danish Champion,' and with each telling he relived, no doubt, the glory of his former days in the ring.

The course was based on the latest information and the training was made as realistic as possible within the limits that safety imposed. Tear gas and choking gases were released at unexpected times and with the minimum of warning. Any

student who was not sufficiently alert when the gas alarm was
given experienced a certain amount of discomfort although it
was not of a permanent or serious nature. The use of phosphorus as an incendiary weapon was now a feature in all large
incendiary bombs and was a dangerous substance for civil
defence workers to contend with. The Northern Ireland civil
defence had not encountered this type of bomb and had no
experience of the effects of phosphorus or how to deal with it.
The task before the demonstration team was to teach the
hazards and methods of dealing with phosphorus fires. The
fire was prepared and phosphorus grenades were exploded to
show how this substance ignited when it came into contact
with the air. The fires were tackled and emphasis was given on
how to avoid undue contamination from the phosphorus. It
was my job to teach awareness and care to prevent contamination and on occasions I deliberately and carelessly wandered
through damp embers as I sprayed them with my stirrup
pump. In due course the fires were extinguished and everything looked harmless. We withdrew and I would walk about
in full view of the students. There would be widespread
excitement and alarm when my boots burst into flames as the
phosphorus dried out and re-ignited. The team always stood
by with their stirrup pumps and soon had the fire under
control before it could do me any harm. This spectacular
exercise did more to press home the lesson than a thousand
words could have accomplished. All the tools were thoroughly
cleaned and the boots were hosed down before they were
packed away. By this time the class understood the danger of
re-ignition.

The class showed great interest in what, to them, was a new
incendiary agent and we involved them in another impressive
exercise. A large pit had been prepared and all the residue
from the fire was carefully buried. During the final lesson at
the end of the course, which was a few days later, this material
was exhumed and in a few minutes it burst into flames and
gave the demonstration team another fire to fight as a finale to
the last training course they would be called upon to attend.

The trainees never knew quite what to expect and as they
moved about in the wild surroundings, with the Cavehill
behind them, they soon became lost in the make believe world

of gas, fires and bombs which we were attempting to unfold before them.

Contrary to popular rumour none of the disguised, small anti-personnel bombs were used during the blitz on Belfast, but they were a weapon that would possibly be used in any future attack. Specialised knowledge was required to search out and identify these nasty little devices. Anti-personnel bombs had a dual purpose and although small they were capable of killing or causing serious injuries. In addition they had a nuisance value and when dropped in large numbers they could disrupt traffic over a wide area or hold up local production. The bombs were dropped in containers similar to those used for dispersing incendiaries.

The Germans used various kinds of this device but their favourite was the Butterfly Bomb. It consisted of a small grenade and it came floating down to earth by means of a small rotating propeller. As well as guiding the bomb gently to the ground, the rotating motion unscrewed a safety catch inside the bomb and activated it. The bombs did not explode on impact but lay around as potential booby traps, primed and ready to explode if disturbed.

It was the duty of the police and wardens to search out and locate them before they caused death or injury. These devices are still causing damage, especially in rural areas where animals and ramblers disturb them while moving across the fields or through the thicket. Each new accident starts another search and war-time memories are recalled as reports of such incidents are reported in the press.

We mounted such searches and taught the safety precautions to be observed in these operations. Models of anti-personnel bombs were hidden in the grass and the bushes, and hung from the guttering of outhouses in a defined area. Some of these models were placed close to wired-up thunder-flashes and watchful members of the demonstration team exploded them if any of the searchers acted carelessly. The offending searcher was declared injured and was withdrawn from the search team. We were sure the embarrassment would drive home to him the necessity of extreme caution. In an actual search the whole team would have retreated carefully along the track they had already searched in case the explosion would have activated the delayed fuses in other bombs in the area, and the search would not have been resumed for a few hours or even the next day. In our case we only stopped for a few minutes and the search was resumed. Search parties spread out in a straight line under the control of a leader. When a suspicious object was discovered the search party was ordered to halt and stand where they were. If a bomb was confirmed its position was indicated by a coloured marker and the location shown on a map of the area. The search continued until all the models were found.

Our search for realism caused some annoyance to a section of the public on one occasion. It was customary to ask for wind directions and clearance from the air ministry at Aldergrove when we intended using gas or smoke canisters. On one particular day there was a sudden change in the wind direction and clouds of gas drifted down on to the Antrim Road. It was a beautiful day and the corporation transport department had a number of open air trams operating on the Bellevue route. The upper deck open air trams were brought into use in the summer and the passengers crowded up the stairs and enjoyed the scenery and the fresh air as the old trams rattled and lumbered slowly out to Bellevue and Glengormley. This area at the time was open country and a favourite picnic ground for the city folk.

This was the setting on the day our exercise went wrong. The drifting clouds of gas enveloped the trams and sent the passengers scurrying to the lower decks, which were more protected by glass windows. Meanwhile we received frantic messages from the police who were busy closing the road and diverting traffic. We did all we could to reduce the cloud by covering the canisters with earth and sandbags. It must have been a terrible experience for those who were caught by the gas that day. It was not a dangerous type of gas but it was very irritating and I am sure frightening.

Finally the course was finished. Every full-time warden had passed through a thorough course of training and had been tested by the various exercises we had staged. They had seen the effects of phosphorus and how to deal with it. There were moments when they were caught in clouds of gas and they had played like children searching for hidden articles. We taught them how to build protective sandbag walls and prepare refuge rooms. All this was done in a pleasant and friendly atmosphere. We knew as we parted that they had enjoyed the instruction. After the war I often met some men and women on the streets who greeted me with the words 'Aren't you the warden from Park Lodge?' It was the only course of its kind and it was adjudged a great success. The opinion of observers from the Ministry was that the success was due to the imagination and efforts of the demonstration team, and later we each received a personal letter of thanks outlining their observations.

The training course was intended for the full-time wardens but the volunteers were kept up to date by the use of film shows, lectures and combined exercises. While the armed forces prepared for the greatest battles in the experience of mankind, the civil defence and fire service had their part to play in the defence of the home front. It was ironic that, in Belfast, the high degree of training came after the worst of the blitz when it would have been of most value.

1944 was certainly a year of decision. The second front, which for the countless thousands in Hitler's occupied Europe, had been a dream and a sign of hope, was now a reality. Everything depended on the outcome of the strategy and fighting power of our forces. Victory was in sight but it was feared that this victory would have to be paid for with the blood of innocent victims at home. The home front had to face the possibility that the enemy would launch a new attack on British cities, using some new destructive weapons, or perhaps gas. This indeed was the German plan and London was to face more nights of terror. The Germans sent flying bombs and rockets in day and night raids right into the following year when the invasion forces destroyed the remaining launching pads in Holland.

Early training at Park Lodge, June 23, 1941.   (Ulster Museum Garland Collection)
Male and female communications staff from report centres, photographed with two wardens and the inevitable stirrup pumps and buckets. The white helmets show that the wardens were officers.

17 Belfast, the last alert

Although we were always conscious of our primary role in relation to the community, Post 381 could in no way be thought of as a place of despondency and gloom. The post was always a cosy and happy place at night. Apart from the full-time staff there were always the regulars who called in for a chat on their way home and we always had at least six volunteers on rota duty to patrol the area. Unlike some groups we encouraged the wardens to use the post as a social centre and not to think of it as a rallying place only in the event of a disaster. The post had a distinctive charm that captivated all who were associated with it. There were never any quarrels or petty jealousies. The wardens were ideally suited for the job they had volunteered to do.

Since the blitz, the patrols were not only for blackout enforcement but also because the residents liked to see the wardens patrolling their streets and they too, as if on a rota, offered them tea and sandwiches during the night. This was the situation on Tuesday 27th June 1944 at 12.07 just after midnight. The babble of conversation was interrupted as the telephone rang. I lifted the receiver and heard the telephonist give the code word for the day in order to establish that the message about to be given was not a hoax. Then came the message, 'Air raid warning', there was a slight pause and then followed the final and most important word of the message 'Red'. That was all: the phone went dead as the telephonist hung up and prepared to transmit her grim message to other posts in the district. All faces were on me as I replaced the receiver. Instinctively they sensed something was wrong.

I had scarcely time to repeat the message when the silence of the night was shattered by the awesome wailing of the sirens.

It is impossible to describe the feelings of fear and terror that the sound of the sirens brought to any community. There is a passage in scripture which says 'Pray that your flight shall not be at night'. Unfortunately, the heaviest raids always happened at night and in the darkness and silence the panic and fear were magnified. There were seven wardens in the post at the time and they started to lay out equipment and message forms for the wardens who would soon be reporting for duty. It was a long time since we had carried out a similar duty on Easter Tuesday in preparation for what turned out to be the most terrifying attack on our city and later during the fire raid. The sound of voices and the sharp bang of doors being closed echoed in the silence of the night as people left their houses and made their way to the shelters. Then we heard the sound of running and hurried footsteps as the first of the wardens reported for duty. In all, 22 wardens reported in that night. There were some whom we had not seen for some time, there were recent recruits and I was more than delighted to see some old hands who had left the neighbourhood but had come back in order to offer their services and experience.

It was a wonderful response. In spite of the lapse of time the sense of duty and the spirit of friendship had not diminished. The knowledge of the danger and destructive power of modern weapons did not deter them. I was the group warden at the time and was in complete control of a large and extended area but I was proud to know that I had such a group of tried and trusted men around me. Yes, they were indeed a grand bunch of fellows and all volunteers.

There was an air of excitement in the room as I briefed the wardens on their duties. I could sense the fear and excitement among the young men and read the minds of the old hands as we discussed our plan of action. A multitude of thoughts passed through my mind at that moment. What would the night bring? Would we again be a target? How would we react if we came under attack? Would we be able to give our best as we had on previous occasions? I prayed that we would. Some of the wardens remained at the post with Alex Boyle, the post warden, and the rest went out into the tense, still night. Every man knew just what was expected of him and as each group broke away from the main party to take up their allotted positions they called out good luck wishes to each other as they disappeared into the darkness.

I knew what their thoughts must have been as I left them. I had tried to balance the patrols by giving a lot of thought to keeping close friends together. People operated best with someone they liked and trusted, but at the same time I had to make sure that I did not allow new or inexperienced recruits to go out without someone to guide them.

The patrols were briefed to check on shelters and see how the shelter marshals were operating. This was their first call to duty since they were recruited and it struck me that they would appreciate our interest in the new service. It also let the people who had taken shelter know that the wardens were patrolling the area and were ready to assist them if necessary.

My old friend Montague was still with the squad and we decided to make a quick tour of the whole post area. The teams of firefighters were already in position. They had their own leaders although wardens had overall control and could call on them or direct them to particular fires in their area. There was close co-operation between the fireguards and our wardens and we were content to give them a free hand at that stage. I was pleased that they had acted on their own initiative and had rallied at the arranged fire points. All that was required was a word of encouragement from myself or another warden if they were called into action. We stopped a few minutes with each group as we went through the streets and arranged to keep in touch. The fire guards outnumbered the wardens and as they were present in practically every street this meant that there was another channel of communication throughout the entire post area. I was instrumental in the organising and training of these firefighters and saw the possibility of involving them in message transmission and communication with the wardens.

The preparations for civil defence to meet any future attack on the city were greatly improved. The equipment of the supporting services was modernised and was more readily available. In my mind I could visualise the plan coming together like a jigsaw puzzle. Out on the streets the wardens were on patrol ready to fulfil their brief to report damage and to bring assistance to the injured or distressed. The chain of

fireguards stretched across the city was part of the plan to meet
the threat of a fire blitz. At the depots fire, rescue and ambulance squads were standing by, waiting for calls from control
centres. As I moved about I saw for the first time the organisation we had built up for the defence of the area during the
previous year. Without any prompting the whole plan had
fallen into place. Everybody knew what they were to do and
they had reported to their positions. Unlike many of us at the
time of the blitz, wardens and fire guards were aware of the
dangers and the need for self-discipline if they were to avoid
them. Above all there was a more settled atmosphere in the
community itself which came as a bonus to the wardens
patrolling the streets. As I observed all this my thoughts
drifted back to the awful nights in 1941 when only a handful of
wardens had worked and made superhuman efforts to save
life and give some assistance to the injured and distressed.

In spite of our inner fears of what the night would bring, we
were content with what we saw. The shelters were greatly
improved and more comfortable. With the destructive power
of bombs now being used, shelters offered at least some
degree of safety to the people. Their own little houses offered
no protection whatsoever to these new weapons and they
would have certainly burned like tinder in the event of widespread fires.

The searchlights sped across the sky, crossing and recross-
ing one another in their continuous search for enemy aircraft.
It was encouraging to see them and know that the anti-aircraft
batteries had been strengthened. We passed the bomb sites,
some of which were already part of local folklore with tales of
the paranormal. Locals avoided these places at night and even
sturdy men were known to take detours when returning home
late at night. The wardens patrolled these areas several times
during the night and early morning but had never seen or
experienced anything unnatural. If such apparitions did
appear, surely this night would have been a suitable time for
such manifestations and had we not been close to the departed
spirits? In many cases we were the first to touch their lifeless
bodies as we helped to remove them from the debris but we
saw nothing.

It was almost an hour since the alert was sounded and we began to feel anxious. 'There must be German planes about somewhere,' we thought. Perhaps there were a few planes that had become detached from a raiding party elsewhere, but even an attack consisting of a few planes armed with new powerful bombs and incendiaries could cause serious damage. These thoughts dispelled all the foolish talk of ghosts and other folklore tales of the neighbourhood. We listened intently and watched the sky for any sign of enemy planes. We had almost completed our tour of the post area when the all clear sounded and as the continuous unbroken sound echoed through the narrow streets we hurried along to join our comrades.

The alert had lasted about an hour and during those sixty minutes memories were recalled and friendships cemented. It was a sad parting that night and some of the wardens were never to return to the post again. For the civil defence it was a time for testing and again it answered the call.

Milburne Henke of Hutchinson, Minnesota, the first American soldier to land in Ulster in the Second World War.

18 An American forces plane crash

For most people the war years were long and dreary and for those engaged in civil defence it became a waiting game. In such circumstances it was difficult to maintain enthusiasm in a voluntary organisation. Post 381 was fortunate in that its deep involvement in all matters pertaining to civil defence kept it fully engaged, and I was often called up to do duties outside my own post area.

One summer day in 1944 a simple but dramatic telephone message came from headquarters. An American airforce plane had crashed behind the Floral Hall at Bellevue and another warden and myself were to report there as soon as possible. The fire and ambulance services had been alerted and were on their way. The location was not part of my normal territory but I was getting used to being sent to different areas at that time. My companion and I picked up our first aid kits and helmets and set out immediately. So started a chain of events which even to this day I find hard to explain completely.

We saw the shocking sight of the crumpled wreckage and when we arrived the ambulance crews and firemen were already at work. We joined the ambulance crews to help take away the bodies. A strict security ring was thrown up and manned by armed American personnel. After the operation was finished we were directed to report to an American officer who asked us to stand by at one of the security posts which were being set up.

We expected to perform some kind of liaison between the guards and the public who were beginning to gather. After the fire engines and ambulances had left, the security became tighter. Barbed wire fences were erected and armed guards took up positions. We watched as American military police with long truncheons started to patrol the area outside the fencing and realised that our services would not be needed in these circumstances. The public were certainly not welcome and would be kept away completely. As there was nothing further for us to do, we asked if we could leave but we were told that for security reasons we could not leave. The officer, with some embarrassment, explained that we were not being detained and that we could move about. He added that we would be permitted to leave as soon as security allowed and again apologised.

Whatever was happening we believed that a few hours would clear it up. It was a beautiful day and we went on a tour of the site trying at all times to keep away from the armed guards. It struck us as strange that we were the only British personnel in the compound. There was no R.A.F., army or police presence and we could not understand how this could be. How was it that two civil defence wardens were the only British representatives in what to our mind was now a declared piece of American territory and we did not like our enforced detention in spite of the repeated apologies of the American officer.

The wreckage of the plane was surrounded by an armed guard. There were papers and broken boxes of emergency rations scattered over a wide area. Among the scattered papers was a writing pad in which there was a partly written letter from one of the crew to his mother. I will always remember the few lines of that letter 'Mother, we are now flying over Ireland and we will be going down in a few minutes'. These words followed by a long wild scrawl of the pen and were the last thoughts of some young airman just before the fatal crash. The Flying Fortress had failed to clear the low ridge just above the Bellevue plateau and crashed into the cliff face. There were no survivors. All those young men who just moments previously were dreaming dreams and making plans were now dead, their bodies burned and mangled amid the mass of twisted metal. The Floral Hall, nearby, escaped damage and stood magnificently marking an area noted for its scenic beauty and festivities. The hillside that day, however, was marred by one of war's disasters.

We took the letter and some photographs which we found to

the officer who had been speaking to us. I have often thought of that letter and hoped that it was delivered. At least it would have brought some solace to a bereaved mother by letting her know that her dear son's last thoughts were of her.

From snippets of conversation, we learned that the plane was fitted with some top secret equipment including a most secret and highly effective bomb-aiming device. Judging from the scale of the security precautions we reckoned that apart from the disaster itself we were involved in something big and we contented ourselves by thinking that at least we would have a good story to tell when we returned home.

It was some time since we had arrived at the incident and wandering about in the mountain air gave us an appetite and suddenly we felt hungry. We did not have any lunch or packed meal with us as we had not expected to be away so long. The Americans were supplied with packed lunches but they did not share these rations with us. We remembered the emergency food packets which were scattered about the hillside and off we went to forage. It was so bizarre. Here we were only a few hundred yards from the main road and civilisation and yet we were forced to scavenge for food as if we were castaways on some far-away uninhabited island. The iron rations consisted of water biscuits, cheese, some kind of dried meat, a packet of five cigarettes and a stimulant powder which we made into a pleasant drink with water from our first aid kits. The iron rations were the only food we had until we returned home the following day.

The Americans we met on our first evening were friendly fellows and they talked about their home towns, their families and their jobs back home. Before their relief came they warned us about a real crazy guy. According to them he was a trigger-happy character whom they avoided at all times. They advised us always to keep him in sight and not to approach him when it was dark. 'This was going to be nice company for us', we thought but at the same time we believed they were only making fun and if there was indeed such a character we would probably find him completely different from how they had described him. However, when he did arrive, we soon learned that they had not been joking after all. When he appeared the fellows we were speaking to left without any

words of greeting or conversation with him. After they had
gone he told us he did not permit anyone to be about the sentry
post and that we were not to come near unless he called us,
and as a parting shot as we moved away he warned us not to
move about in the dark. By this time in spite of the original
American officer's assurances we felt that we were indeed
prisoners under the supervision of a crazy guard who never let
go of his service revolver. It was a warm, sultry night and as
darkness set in we stretched out within his vision and fell
asleep on the grassy hillside.

Morning came and the fresh relief sentry asked us how we
got on. Some other fellows joined us on their way to take up
duty at other posts and the sentry was eager to tell them how
we had passed the night with the 'Crazy Guy'. This was the
name applied to him throughout the unit and not, as we had
believed, one made up by the fellows who had told us about
him the previous evening. When we explained how we had
passed the night, one of them said 'You sure did the right
thing. That guy is the craziest I've seen in this goddam Army.'
'He's shot more of our guys than the Germans,' said another.
Apparently he had wounded several fellows sneaking back
into camp at night and had made deliberate shots at others to
frighten them.

The soldiers moved on and we were alone again except for
the lone sentry left at the post. There was still no sign of food
being brought to us so we went off again to forage among the
scattered debris from the plane for some more emergency food
packets. We unearthed several unbroken packets and a few
cans of fruit juice. As we settled down to breakfast I started to
laugh. My companion looked at me with a puzzled expression
and it struck me that perhaps he was thinking that the strain of
the night was too much for me and that I was cracking up. The
sudden thought only tended to make me laugh all the more.
'What's the matter, Doc?' he asked in a serious tone of voice.
'There's nothing the matter,' I replied, 'I was only thinking
about what the American authorities would say if they could
see us, two hungry Belfast wardens eating these American
rations on an open hillside somewhere in Northern Ireland.'
The thought must have amused him also because he almost
choked with laughter. 'And I thought you were going kind of

soft,' he spluttered as a few crumbs of the biscuits caught in his throat.

The morning was well on before work began in earnest on the plane. A bunch of technicians accompanied by a group of top brass arrived on the scene. There was a lot of activity in and about the plane as teams of men searched through the wreckage and the immediate surroundings. Sensing that security was being tightened up and not wishing to become involved with the new guards we withdrew to some distance and watched the activity around the plane. Although we still resented our unlawful detention at least the situation was somewhat more interesting now. Throughout the previous evening and early morning, especially when we were under the surly gaze of the unfriendly security guard, there had been nothing for us to do but sit around and stare down the slope towards the main road. We were glad that we had been able to forage around for some more food for breakfast before the search operation started but now as the day went on we were feeling hungry again. We dare not risk going towards where the emergency rations were scattered. They were too close to the plane and the guards now on duty struck us as being no less crazy than the character with whom we had passed the night. It was better to be hungry than dead or seriously wounded, we thought, because we felt it was likely that those trigger-happy Yankee guards would have shot at anything that moved.

From our vantage point we had to be content with passing the time by watching the technicians working on the plane. From what we could see they dismantled parts, while those engaged in searching picked up pieces of metal and other objects from the scattered debris of the plane. All this material was placed carefully in a small truck which moved off with an armed escort. The heavy squad then took over and started to load the wreckage on to a large carrier. It was about four o'clock in the afternoon when the work was completed. The security fencing was dismantled and stacked with tools and other equipment on to another truck. The remaining Americans climbed into a couple of jeeps and waved to us as they drove off and disappeared in the enveloping dust which they threw up all around them.

The hillside was deserted and now seemed strange to us. We had become accustomed to looking at the massive fuselage of the plane and watching the activities of the American servicemen, now we were alone on the hillside with only a large gap in the crushed bushes and ploughed up earth to mark the scene of the disaster.

Away from the watchful eyes of our guards, the feeling of restriction was replaced by one of inquisitiveness and we started to search around for some souvenirs. Under the circumstances it was fitting that we should be the first among the souvenir hunters. By this time we were really hungry and we broke open a few of the packets of iron rations that now lay in abundance close to where the plane had crashed. We sat down and enjoyed a good meal before we left for home. The food was pleasant and the circumstances surrounding it made the meal both interesting and exciting. I sat and gazed around this historic setting as we ate and thought of the stories of the Seven Giants and other folklore about the Cave Hill that I had read or heard of as a boy. Behind me was the setting for another tale to be added to the folklore of the hill. As time passes by, perhaps the story will be told of how the Seven Giants, the guardians of the Cave Hill, did battle with a ferocious flying giant and threw it to the ground. For us, however, it was another story in the history of Post 381. It was time to leave and we gathered up some more food packets and souvenirs for the wardens at the post and made our way down the hill. The wire fencing and the guards were all away and as we descended we met a crowd of sightseers and souvenir hunters making their way towards what remained of the wreckage.

'There'll be very little left of the wreckage or anything else when that gang are finished,' I said. 'Wreckage! that gang will take the very grass,' was the reply.

Our prolonged absence and the lack of news as to our whereabouts caused concern to our families and our comrades at the post. Two wardens had gone to enquire about us but the guards had turned them away after telling them that we were inside the security circle somewhere and that we were all right. I sent a full report of the incident to headquarters and although I raised the matter on several occasions I never received a satisfactory answer. The incident still puzzles me. Was our detention due to overreaction by the security guards?

There was a sequel to the story about 35 years later when my memory was jogged by a letter which appeared in the *Belfast Telegraph* from someone in Canada, and the writer sought to hear from anyone who had information about the crash. I wrote to him and received a very interesting letter in reply.

He had been at the scene of the crash with some young friends and tried to take away part of the wreckage as a souvenir. An American military policeman had chased them off. Later he tried to find out about the crash from the American airforce but they came up with nothing. He had tried again in the 1970s to make further investigations, while visiting Belfast, but he could not even find anyone who could locate the site. He was grateful to me for letting him know my experiences.

Perhaps we will never find out exactly why the plane crashed and what was the reason for the extreme secrecy.

Post 381, winners of the Hayes Cup
(See pages 122–3). Front row, left to right: James Doherty (the author), Alex Boyle (kneeling in front), William Trainor, Rev McKinney (guest), Brian Gillespie (Group Warden), Fr Richard O'Neill (guest), Dennis Kelly and John Montague.

(Doherty Collection)

19 Northern Ireland wardens in London

The Allied invasion of occupied Europe and the final defeat of Nazi Germany was, at this time, becoming a reality for the millions who were suffering at the hands of the Nazis. Simultaneously in the summer of 1944 London and the south east coast became the targets for the German's new secret weapons. The flying bomb or V1 was a pilotless plane with a heavy explosive charge in the nose. It was propelled by a form of alcoholic spirit and was fitted with a device which cut out the motor after a certain number of revolutions were made. It was not a guided missile but a terror weapon. It had no electronic apparatus to guide it and the Germans had no control over it after it was launched. The best they could expect was that it would land somewhere inside the target area.

The bombs came flying in by day and by night. London was in a constant state of alert. The bombs flew at a speed of over 400 miles per hour and although many where shot down over the channel, thousands reached their target. The civil defence services were under call continuously and urgently needed rest. A call went out for help to other authorities throughout the country and Northern Ireland was one of the regions called upon.

I volunteered and was accepted. A team of about thirty experienced wardens left Belfast early in September 1944 but due to strict censorship there was no mention of the departure in the press and to my knowledge this is the first full report of the Northern Ireland civil defence serving in London during the flying bomb and rocket attacks.

We arrived at Euston Station on a wet and blustery Saturday afternoon. I don't know what I expected but I do know that I experienced no joy from what was my first sight of London.

161

The atmosphere was drab and the station and the immediate surroundings bore the scars that had been inflicted on the city during the long years of the war. We were met by some local officials who brought us to a tea kiosk run by the Salvation Army where we had tea and sandwiches. We were grateful for the meal and hot tea. The crossing to Stranraer had been rough and the subsequent rail journey on a crowded train took up to fourteen hours, most of which was spent sitting on the floor on our kit bags. There were other wardens at the station from Yorkshire and Bristol. They, too, had to travel under cramped conditions and like ourselves were cold and hungry.

There had been a lot of activity during the night and our transport was delayed. We must have stood about in the rain for two hours or more. Even in the shelter of the station the rain continued to fall through the large roof now devoid of glass. It was around four o'clock when a number of fire service personnel carriers arrived. We were split into groups according to pre-arranged lists and finally we were on our way to our allotted locations.

On making inquiries as to where we were going, I was told that we were going to a depot in Richmond, Surrey. The question was asked merely as a piece of conversation and the information that we were on our way to Richmond meant nothing to me except that I recalled my schooldays and associated it with a history lesson about Hampton Court. As we drove along we could see some of the results of the widespread bombing that London had suffered over a period of five years. We passed bomb scarred buildings and the burned out shells of factories, office blocks and large areas laid waste. Our informant added that these were not the worst affected parts of the city.

As we passed by more and more empty spaces I tried to fit the scene into my own experiences. What had the empty spaces meant in human suffering and broken bodies? I could visualize the firemen as they stood grimfaced and fought in vain to contain the blazing infernos. I could see the wardens as they moved about in the glow of the spreading fires and somewhere up in the clouds I imagined that I could hear the drone of enemy bombers.

My day dreaming came to an end as the driver turned into a

large complex and announced that we had arrived. This was the headquarters of the Richmond Rescue Service. A sloping pathway led us down underground where the living quarters were located. It consisted of a canteen, recreation rooms, lecture hall, toilets, showers and sleeping accommodation.

The arrangements were that we would do our normal hours of duty at one of the wardens' posts in the area and we were to sleep and have our meals at the depot. Our off duty hours we could use as we wished. We could use the recreation facilities with the rescue crews or go out into the town. At the depot we met wardens from Wales and Yorkshire and immediately we found ourselves at one with them. We had no difficulty in mixing and in no time it appeared as if we were all members of the same post in our own respective areas.

Work at the post was routine. The problems of the locals were of a similar pattern to those we encountered back home and I dealt with them as I would have done back in Belfast. They must have been pleased with the way I listened to them and the advice I gave, because they came back to see me and some of them brought their friends. It soon got around who I was and it was comical to hear them refer to me as the Irish boy in their rich Richmond accent. There were not many Irish in the Richmond borough and my accent and stories must have held a certain charm for them and a distraction from the humdrum monotony of wartime life. They treated me well and brought me apples and pears from their own gardens and I was invited to a wedding and two 21st birthday parties during my term of duty. The rescue crews at the depot whooped it up when they heard of me being invited to a wedding. 'Ach, sure it must be me Irish blarney,' I replied.

Life was not all fun during that spell of duty and twice I was caught up in explosions. This new type of aerial bombardment did not have the same dangers as an ordinary raid for those working on the ground in the open. The target area was large and the bombs were scattered. It was reasonably safe to work without giving thought to the danger of other bombs coming down as was so often the case with conventional bombing.

The civil defence and the Londoners became used to the flying bombs and adapted themselves to the daily harassment. During the day they could be seen flying in from the coast like

a squadron of planes. The distance they travelled was controlled by the amount of fuel they carried or by a cut-out device
which shut off the fuel supply after a predetermined number
of revolutions on the counting mechanism was registered. The
engine then stopped and they acted like a glider. Sometimes
they dived immediately while others glided on for miles. It
was the glider effect which thrilled those who watched them
the most. The public developed the habit of standing and
watching these monster bombs as they flew overhead. It was
an amazing sight and I often watched them myself. The tense
moments came when the engine cut out, especially if it was
directly above or coming towards you: it was then that there
was a scurry for shelter.

At night it was more frightening to see them in flight. They
could be traced as they raced across the sky at over 400 miles
per hour, with a tail of flame shooting from them like a comet.
It was indeed a thrilling experience to watch these flame
throwing monsters as they shot across the night sky. Our
curiosity and attraction for watching at night was always
accompanied by some apprehension when the flame went out
and the glider was no longer visible. We were familiar with the
habits of the Doodle-bugs as the Londoners had nicknamed
them and in the darkness the watchers sought immediate
shelter until the thunderous crash or explosion was heard.
Soon afterwards, if the bomb came down in our area, the call
would come into the operations room and the rescue crews
would move out.

The depot fire teams operated on similar lines to that of a
rescue station. The crews were on constant alert and answered
calls just as the peace time fire service now do as a regular part
of their duty. It must be remembered that London was facing
not attacks at intervals like Belfast but was facing a bombardment by day as well as night for months on end. I went out
with them on several occasions during my off duty hours.
They were a great bunch of blokes and highly skilled. I learned
a lot from them both in skills and operational control which as
an officer in the St John Ambulance I was able to put into good
use many years later at bombing incidents involving heavy
loss of life and casualties during the troubles in Northern
Ireland.

The flying bombs were designed to cause the maximum blast effect and damage was spread over a wide area. In closely built industrial areas one of these bombs could wreck a few streets. Casualty figures were high and many thousands were killed or seriously wounded during the period.

One particular incident involved the Guards' Chapel at Wellington Barracks. A ceremony at the chapel was in progress when the bomb crashed down. Over 200 guardsmen and visiting dignitaries were killed in this one incident.

Worse, however, was to come. The V2 rocket was a new and terrible weapon which was to bring fear, death and destruction to the south of England. They were used for the first time during our term of duty. These massive bombs were 46 feet in length and carried over a ton of explosives in the nose. They were launched from Holland and had a range of 200 miles. On being launched they rose to a height of 50 or 60 miles and attained a speed of 3,500 m.p.h. The rockets came hurtling from the sky and on account of their tremendous speed no warning of their approach could be given and the population at large was the target for this terror weapon. The rockets, like the flying bombs, came by day and night, stretching the civil defence sevices to their limits. Housewives standing in queues or out shopping became victims. One outstanding incident involved a shopping area being blasted. It was about 11 o'clock in the morning and there were large queues outside the shops when a rocket came crashing down. Some three hundred people were killed and the buildings themselves became a mountain of rubble.

The first rocket to hit the London area landed at about a quarter to seven on the evening of September 8th 1944 at Chiswick, and the attacks continued until invading Allied forces overran the launching sites in March 1945. I was returning to the depot that evening after my spell of duty at the post when I was struck by a strong gust of wind. It came so suddenly and forcefully that it knocked me off my balance and I fell to the ground. There was no warning siren of approaching flying bombs. I thought it was an unexploded bomb that had gone off somewhere nearby, although I did not hear any explosion. Branches and leaves were torn from the trees and fell around me as I lay on the ground. I got up and looked around. I was alone. The avenue remained silent with only the scattered branches and leaves to convince me that something extraordinary had occurred. It was a select residential area with large houses sitting back in their own grounds and as there was no sound of an explosion but only a freak blast effect the residents were unaware of the incident. It turned out that Chiswick, a few miles away, was the site of the mysterious explosion and the fact that slates and chimney pots were dislodged in our own immediate area led to excited discussion and speculation as to what caused so violent an explosion.

Later that night we learned the answer, although not officially, that a new and more powerful weapon, the much feared and expected long range rocket the V2, had at last been launched in the final attack on London.

Although the air force and intelligence service had done much to thwart or delay the rocket attack programme and had suffered severe losses in the battle, the public and the civil defence forces were not aware of the dangers and death and destruction they were to endure for another six months or more. Even with knowledge there was nothing short of bombing the rocket centres and other facilities which could have been done. Unlike the flying bombs there was no defence against the rocket. It was too quick to be seen and monitored and so no warning of its approach could be given.

Censorship clamped down strictly on all reports relating to the rockets and some days passed before the government admitted that German rockets had successfully landed and caused damage. In the early attacks involving rockets, such incidents were reported as gas main explosions or delayed action bombs. In this way the government attempted to keep the public and German intelligence unaware of the widespread damage to property and the mounting death toll. The enemy had to be deprived of any information about the effects of the new weapon or the locations where they landed. The government's plan was to confuse the enemy and make them believe that the rockets were falling short of their target and that little damage was being done. It was also important that the morale of the nation should not be shaken at this crucial point in the conflict.

In spite of strict censorship the Londoners sensed that they were facing a new danger. There had been too many reports of gas mains explosions and, although there was no official advice, they started to go to the shelters again. Those who had Anderson shelters made them as comfortable as possible and retired to them at night. The population went about their business and hurried home. Although the rockets did not arrive in the numbers that were expected, nevertheless for the Londoners it was a time of fear and anxiety. The husband who left home in the morning could not be sure if his wife and family would be alive when he returned nor could he be sure that he himself would return safely.

The warhead of the rocket and the flying bomb contained the same weight of explosive but the rocket claimed twice as many casualties. This was no doubt because the flying bomb could be detected and some warning given, but the rockets crashed down at all times of the day without any warning.

I stopped one night with some friends in Walthamstow and when it came to the time to retire they wanted me to share their shelter. They assured me that it was dangerous to stay in the house as we were in a target area and that there had been much damage caused already. The shelter was a small one suitable for one family only. I did not wish to disturb them and said I would remain in the house. My bedroom windows were draped with heavy curtains. The blackout precautions were complete and when I put out the lights my room was plunged into complete darkness. I fell asleep quickly as I was tired and I was used to sleeping in different places. Suddenly I was awakened by the sound of falling masonry, the screeching of splintered timber and the tinkling of glass. I did not hear the explosion but perhaps it was that which wakened me. My legs and lower part of my body were trapped under the weight of the rubble which continued to fall on me. The darkness of the room enveloped me like a huge blanket and prevented me from seeing anything. My mouth was full of dust and mortar and I felt myself gasping for breath as I went into a spasm of coughing and choking. Panic gripped me as I thought I was buried alive. Thankfully, the panic lasted only a few seconds although it seemed like an eternity.

I calmed down and with my self control back again I realised that my hands were free. I shook off the debris that was holding my arms and reached for the pull switch for the light. I pulled it but there was no light. My thoughts were becoming clearer and it came to me that the heavy mass lying on my legs and stomach and pinioning me down was the massive chandelier and the beautiful ornate plasterwork which I had admired before I put out the light.

I heard hurried footsteps on the stairs and my friend pushed his way into the room holding a flashlamp. I can still recall that ray of light and often in the darkness of my own room I can see again that small, shadowy light and recall what it meant to me one night in London so many years ago.

'Are you all right?' he called as he rushed into the room. 'I think so,' I said. 'If my legs are not damaged.'

By this time he was at my side and was pulling the chandelier and heavy masonry off my legs. I scrambled out of the bed and stepped nervously on to the floor. I breathed a prayer of thanks. My legs were sore and bruised but they were all in one piece. I was none the worse for my experience.

We went downstairs. The rooms were in a mess. The ceilings were down and the windows were wrenched from the brickwork and lay shattered on the ground. The real damage was in the street behind us where the houses were completely demolished. Ten people were killed and dozens injured in the incident that I just narrowly escaped. The damage was severe and had it not been for the Anderson shelters the casualty figures would have been greater. The Londoners owed a lot to these shelters and to the underground railway stations. But like many at home in Belfast, there were those who refused to go to shelters and those were the ones who suffered.

This was the pattern of life at the time for the Londoners. Every day and every night without warning, death visited some part of London. Every family lived under threat. The whole Metropolitan area was under attack. It was a difficult time for the Londoners. Just as victory was within reach they were subjected to a new and terrifying type of attack. Humour came to their aid and they mocked the weapons Hitler hoped would bring him victory. They nicknamed the flying bomb the Doodle-bug and as for the rockets they tried to forget them and renewed the old slogan, 'Business as usual'.

I have one more memory of my stay in Richmond which is far removed from thoughts of war and all its accompanying miseries. Someone at the post asked me if I had been to Kew Gardens and explained how I could get there. My total knowledge of Kew Gardens was contained in a poem I had learned at school. 'Down to Kew in lilac time: Down to Kew in lilac time: Down to Kew in lilac time: it isn't far from London,' which was one of my favourite poems. The poet described it as a veritable wonderland with settings of fairyland scenes and natural beauty. I took the first opportunity to visit Kew and like the poet I was captivated by its beauty.

I lived all my life in a built-up industrial area where even a small garden was a rarity and I had little knowledge of flowers, trees or shrubs. Nevertheless, I was fascinated by their variety and colour and I spent some hours wandering around. I visited the famous glasshouse with its collection of tropical plants and learned that many of them were grown from seeds and that Kew was one of the foremost botanical research stations in the world. There were many other wonders such as the pagoda and restaurant, giant trees and a multitude of birds. I became so engrossed with everything that I lost my bearings and had some difficulty in retracing my steps.

I made two more visits to Kew Gardens before leaving Richmond. I was fascinated by the place and the attraction has remained with me as a lasting memory.

The time spent in London was a great experience for us all. To each of us it brought personal memories. Our term of duty was finished at the end of the month and it was time to return home. In some way by our presence we must have contributed something to the as yet unwritten story of the war on the Home Front.

As a parting gesture we all received the following letter of thanks from the Richmond wardens:

Please accept my thanks and that of the Wardens of this Borough for so readily volunteering to come to Richmond in order to help us during the trying period when we are doing our best to cope with the Flying Bombs.

Please be assured that your public spirited action is very much appreciated and I hope you will return to your home

town feeling that you take with you the friendship and
fellowship of the Richmond Wardens.

H. A. Leon
Chief Warden

This letter sums up the reason for our being in London and the
close friendship which we built up with the wardens and
people and their appreciation of our assistance.

We assembled again at Euston Station. It was an emotional
reunion for the various groups which formed the reinforcing
party. Each group was happy to know that none of their
comrades had suffered injury. Scattered throughout the different boroughs it was possible that had any of our comrades
been injured we would not have known anything about it.

We chatted and exchanged stories as we waited for trains
and then it was all over. Our journey home was uneventful.
We started a sing-song on board the boat in which other
passengers joined. None of us went to bed that night although
we had sleeping berths booked. It was our last night together
and before parting at the docks we agreed to try and arrange a
future meeting. Of course such occasions always give rise to
the sentimental desire for a future reunion but, as these things
happen, we never did get together again. There were, however, chance meetings in the most unexpected places and
these, as would be expected, were occasions for surprise,
emotional handshakes and, of course, reminiscences.

Shortly after my return I was asked to speak about my
experiences at a social evening organised by district headquarters. There was a large turnout, as many of the members
brought along their friends and they were all eager to hear a
report at first hand of conditions in London and to hear some
authoritative information about Hitler's secret weapons.

They were a great audience and I had no bother eliciting
questions from them. They came at me from all sides and I
enjoyed the barrage of queries. They kept me alert and the
question time proved as interesting as the talk itself. It was to
be my last address to a war time audience and a fitting parting
memory. Even as I spoke I knew that my days of lecturing,
training and organising were coming to a close and I was
thankful that it would no longer be needed.

A new spirit was springing up among the population. They could sense the feeling of security and the freedom from fear. For the first time in years they could go to bed and enjoy a good night's sleep. They were no longer constantly haunted by the fear of enemy planes which still, nevertheless, remained a recurring nightmare for many of them. Northern Ireland perhaps experienced this relaxation and freedom from the grip of fear earlier than the rest of Great Britain where they continued to be under attack from occasional raiders, and London was to endure the rocket and flying bomb attacks for another six months.

The feeling spread to the civil defence and like the early days of the Phoney War it began to lose its sense of purpose and drive. At the post the wardens were drifting. The regulars who for years had kept up a nightly vigil now only came in at the weekends.

I knew my work was finished and I was relieved. The job was at times dangerous, exciting and interesting. It had, however, been a heavy responsibility for a young man to carry. I was still only 24. But always I had the support and loyalty of a great team of dedicated comrades. Now, however, I was alone. The wardens who had stood with me on the bomb sites were scattered. I was the last of the original group of wardens who had stood so proudly in line with our new helmets, respirators and armbands before we went out on our first blackout patrol.

Many changes had taken place since that night. I had witnessed death on a large scale. I had seen sorrow, distress, fear and panic in a way very few have had the occasion to see. I saw whole families wiped out and saw the streets I had played in as a child disappear under the weight of bombs or spreading fires. On the credit side I gained an experience beyond value. I learned about people.

As civil defence came to a close there remained a good deal of clerical work to be undertaken. I became engaged in stock-taking and the preparation of reports for the various posts in the district. It may seem strange, but after four years we were still dealing with enquiries from solicitors and other bodies. Indeed I found myself dealing with such queries long after the war. But stores and clerical work held no interest for me. They were far removed from my reasons for joining civil defence and I decided to return to my own line of work.

On October the 8th 1944 I signed on duty for the last time. My work as an Air Raid Warden was finished but Post 381 will always remain part of the lives of those who contributed to its honour.